Luke

To the Lovers of God

THE
PASSION™
TRANSLATION

Translated from the Greek and Aramaic Texts
Dr. Brian Simmons

5 Fold Media
Visit us at www.5foldmedia.com

Endorsement

Brian Simmons is a brilliant man that has been given revelation and insight into a deeper meaning of the Scriptures. God has breathed a passion in Brian to see the rich words of the gospel of Luke presented to us in a new light. In reading this translation of Luke, "To the Lovers of God," your heart, mind, and spirit are summoned into the essence of Christ Jesus' undeniable love for you. I highly recommend this new Bible translation to everyone.

- Dr. Ché Ahn, Senior Pastor of HRock Church in Pasadena, CA
President, Harvest International Ministry
International Chancellor, Wagner Leadership Institute

Translator's Introduction

You are about to read the biography of a wonderful Man, Jesus Christ, written by a physician named Luke. This is the glorious gospel penned by one of His early followers. All four Gospels in our New Testament are inspired by God, but Luke's gospel is unique and distinct. It has been described as the loveliest book ever written. I have to agree.

We know little about the human author. He was a companion of the Apostle Paul for some of his missionary journeys and may have been one of Paul's early converts. Luke was possibly the only non-Jewish writer of the New Testament. Others believe that he was a notable Gentile Christian who gave up everything to follow Jesus and serve His kingdom. Near the end of the Apostle Paul's life, when he was facing martyrdom, Paul wrote of his trusted friend, "Only Luke is with me." 2 Timothy 4:11 (KJV).

This world is a far better place because of the revelation Luke shares with us in his gospel and in Acts. He gave us a very full picture of Jesus' life and ministry, and applied scrupulous accuracy to all he wrote to ensure that what we read was factual. In fact, Luke uses the Greek word for "autopsy" (1:2) for investigating with firsthand knowledge those who had seen what Jesus did and heard what Jesus taught. Dr. Luke performed an "autopsy" on the facts, tracing each of them back to their source to make sure that what he compiled was of the highest degree of accuracy.

Luke, being a physician, learned early, the need to exhibit compassion and mercy toward others. It comes through in every chapter. Luke's gospel is perhaps the most compassionate and love filled account of Jesus' life ever written.

Luke provides us with rich details of Jesus' love of children, and of the forsaken. Luke writes more about Jesus' ministry to women than the other three gospel authors. Keep this in mind because this was somewhat controversial in the culture of his day. In fact, Luke uses an alternating narrative throughout—one story is about a man, and then the next is about a woman. Luke begins with the story of Zechariah, and then moves to Mary. He focuses on Simeon, then on Anna. Next comes the Roman centurion, then the widow of Nain—followed by the Good Samaritan, then Mary and Martha. This beautiful pattern moves consecutively throughout his gospel.

Luke shares Jesus' teachings on prayer, forgiveness, and of our obligation to demonstrate mercy and grace in our dealings with others. Luke's pen was anointed by the Holy Spirit and his book is still read today by the lovers of God, because it is the "mercy gospel." It is a book for everybody—for everyone needs mercy.

Luke writes clearly of the humanity of Jesus—as the servant *of* all, and the sacrifice *for* all. Every barrier is broken down in Luke's gospel between Jew and Gentile, men and women, rich and poor. We see Jesus in Luke as the Savior of all who come to Him.

A large amount of Luke's gospel is not found in any other gospel narrative. If we did not have Luke, we wouldn't know about the stories of the Prodigal Son, the Good Samaritan, the wedding banquet, and many other amazing teachings! It is only in the book of Luke that we find the stories of the shepherds at Bethlehem, the ten lepers who were healed, and the dying thief on the cross next to Jesus. How thankful I am for the gospel of Luke!

As a missionary translator, Luke was the first New Testament book that I helped translate. It is fitting that once again, it is the first book translated from the New Testament into The Passion Translation. My heart overflows with the joy of seeing this dream realized, of the Word of God being translated, with all of its passion and fire, into contemporary English. I set before you this imperfect, but passionate, attempt to give you the same "thrill" that overwhelmed the first century readers when they heard the story of Jesus Christ for the first time and without a religious filter.

Unveiled before your eyes will be the glorious Man, Jesus Christ, and the revelation of His undying love for you! Allow all of Him to touch all your needs today, and you will never be disappointed! I present to you, and to every lover of God, the gospel of *Luke!*

Brian Simmons

Luke 1

¹⁻⁴Dear Lover of God,

I am writing for you, my honorable friend,* an orderly account of what Jesus Christ accomplished and fulfilled among us. Several eyewitness biographies have already been written† using as their source material the good news preached among us by Christ's early disciples, who became loving servants of the Manifestation.‡ But now I am passing on to you this accurate compilation of my own meticulous investigation§ based on numerous eyewitness interviews and thorough research of the story of His life. It is appropriate for me to write this, for He also appeared to me¶ so that I would reassure you beyond any shadow of a doubt the reliability of all you have been taught of Him.

The Birth of the Prophet John

⁵It begins when Herod the Great was king over Judea. There was a Jewish priest in those days named Zechariah** who served in the temple as part of the priestly order of Abijah.†† His wife, Elizabeth‡‡, was also from a family of priests, being a direct descendant of Aaron. ⁶They were both lovers of God, living virtuously and following the commandments of the Lord fully. ⁷But they were childless since Elizabeth was barren, and now they both were quite old.

* The Greek text is literally, "most excellent Theophilus." The name *Theophilus* means "friend of God" or "lover of God." Many scholars believe that the Theophilus mentioned in Luke's writings was not a real person. This becomes instead, a greeting to all the lovers of God.
† It is likely that Matthew and Mark are the two gospel accounts Luke refers to here.
‡ Translated literally from the Aramaic text. The Greek word is *logos.*
§ The Greek word used here is actually the equivalent of our word *autopsy,* "to see with the eye."
¶ Translated literally from the Aramaic text. The Greek text uses the same term for "coming from above" found in John 3:31, and 19:11. Luke is revealing that the Lord Jesus appeared to him and authorized him to compile his inspired gospel.
** *Zechariah* means "God has remembered."
†† King David organized the priests into twenty-four divisions and Abijah was the head of one of the priestly families. See Nehemiah 12:12, 17 and 1 Chronicles 24:10.
‡‡ *Elizabeth* means "oath," or "covenant of God."

7

8-9One day while Zechariah's priestly order was on duty, and he was serving as priest, it just so happened that by the casting of lots (according to the custom of the priesthood), the honor fell upon Zechariah to enter into the Holy Place* and burn incense before the Lord. 10A large crowd of worshippers had gathered to pray outside the temple at the hour when incense was being offered. 11All at once an angel of the Lord appeared to him standing just to the right of the altar of incense!†

12Zechariah was startled and overwhelmed with fear. 13But the angel reassured him, saying, "Don't be afraid, Zechariah! God is gracious to you!‡ For I have come to tell you that your prayer for a child, a prayer you don't even pray anymore§, has been answered! Your wife Elizabeth will bear you a son and you are to name him, John! 14His birth will bring you much joy and gladness. Many will rejoice because of him. 15He will be one of the great ones in the sight of God. He will drink no wine or strong drink,¶ but he will be filled with the Holy Spirit even while still in his mother's womb. 16And he will persuade many in Israel to convert and turn back to the Lord their God. 17He will go before the Lord as a forerunner, with the same power and anointing of Elijah the prophet! He will be instrumental in turning the hearts of the fathers in tenderness back to their children and the hearts of the disobedient back to the wisdom of their righteous fathers. And he will prepare a united people** who are ready for the Lord's appearing."

18Zechariah asked the angel, "How do you expect me to believe this? I'm an old man and my wife is too old to give me a child. What sign can you give me to prove this will happen?" ††

19Then the angel said, "I am Gabriel! I stand beside God Himself! He has sent me to you to announce this good news! 20But now, since you did not believe my words, you will be stricken silent and unable to speak‡‡ until

---

* There are said to have been twenty thousand priests in Christ's time, so that no priest would ever offer incense more than once. This was a once in a lifetime moment for him! The burning of incense before the Lord was done twice daily—once in the morning and once in the afternoon (Exodus 30:7-8).
† This would be the South side of the temple, between the altar of incense and the golden lampstand.
‡ Implied in the context and in the name *John*, which means, "God is gracious."
§ Or, "a prayer you don't even pray anymore."
¶ Most likely, John was to be a Nazarite from birth—one totally set apart for God and who would fulfill the Nazarite vow found in Numbers 6:1-12.
** Implied in the text. The words "united people" are found in the Aramaic text.
†† Implied in the text.
‡‡ Since Zechariah asked for a sign rather than believe the word of the Lord, he was given the sign of silence. Unbelief keeps a priest from speaking until faith arises.

the day my words have been fulfilled at their appointed time and a child is born to you. That will be your sign!"

²¹Meanwhile, the crowds outside kept expecting him to come out. They were amazed over Zechariah's delay* wondering what could have happened inside the sanctuary. ²²When he finally did come out, he tried to talk but he couldn't speak a word, and they realized from his gestures that he had seen a vision while in the Holy Place! ²³He remained mute as he finished his days of priestly ministry in the temple and then went back to his own home. ²⁴Soon afterwards his wife, Elizabeth, became pregnant and went into seclusion for the next five months. ²⁵She said with joy, "See how kind it is of God to gaze upon me,† and take away the disgrace of my barrenness!"

Angelic Prophecy of Jesus' Birth

²⁶⁻²⁷During the sixth month of Elizabeth's pregnancy, the angel Gabriel was sent from God's presence to an unmarried girl‡ named Mary, living in Nazareth,§ a village in Galilee.¶ She was engaged **to a man named Joseph, a true descendant of King David. ²⁸Gabriel appeared to her and said, "Grace to you, young woman, for you are anointed with great favor, and our Master is with you! "††

²⁹Mary was shocked over the words of the angel and perplexed over what this may mean for her. ³⁰But the angel reassured her saying, "Don't yield to your fear, Mary, for the Lord has found delight in you and has chosen to surprise you with a wonderful gift. ³¹You will become pregnant with a baby boy, and you are to name Him, 'Jesus'! ³²He will be Supreme‡‡ and will be known as the Son of the Highest! And the Lord God will enthrone

---

* They were waiting outside for the priest to come out and speak over them the customary Aaronic blessing found in Numbers 6:24-26.

† This phrase is translated from the Aramaic text.

‡ Many translations have the word *virgin* as a possible translation of the Greek word *parthenos*, but its most common usage implies a girl of marriageable age. It is made explicit in Matthew 1:25 and Luke 1:34 that Mary was indeed a virgin.

§ *Nazareth* means"branch." Jesus grew up as the Branch of the Lord in the city of the branch.

¶ The Aramaic word for Galilee means, "revealed." It is fitting that God would first be "revealed" in the village of Galilee.

** This betrothal period usually lasted one year and unfaithfulness on the part of the bride during the engagement was punishable by death.

†† For Gabriel to say, "Our Master is with you," signifies that Jesus, our Master, was now conceived in her womb. This is what bewildered Mary.

‡‡ As translated from the Aramaic text.

Him as King on His ancestor David's throne. [33]He will reign as King of Israel* forever and His reign will have no limit!"

[34]Mary said, "But how could this happen? I am still a virgin!"

[35]Gabriel answered, "The Spirit of Holiness will fall upon you and the Almighty God will spread His shadow of power over you in a cloud of glory![†] This is why the child born to you will be holy,[‡] and He will be called the Son of God! [36]What's more, your aged aunt,[§] Elizabeth, has also became pregnant with a son. The 'barren one' is now in her sixth month! [37]No promise from God is empty of power, for with God there is no such thing as impossibility!"[¶]

[38]Then Mary responded, saying, "This is amazing! I will be a mother for the Lord!** As His servant, I accept whatever He has for me! May everything you have told me come to pass." And the angel left her.

Elizabeth's Prophecy to Mary

[39]Afterwards, Mary arose and hurried off to the hill country of Judea, to the village where Zechariah and Elizabeth lived. [40]Arriving at their home, Mary entered the house and greeted Elizabeth. [41]At the very moment she heard Mary's voice, the baby within Elizabeth's womb jumped and kicked! And suddenly, Elizabeth was filled to overflowing with the Holy Spirit! [42]With a loud voice she began to prophesy with power,[††]

> "Mary! You are a woman with the highest favor
> And privilege above all others!
> For your child is destined to bring God great delight!
> [43]How did I deserve such a remarkable honor

---

* Or, "house of Jacob."

† The Greek word used as a metaphor, and translated "spread His shadow of power," is the word also used at Jesus' transfiguration when the cloud of glory "overshadowed" Jesus on the mountain (Mark 9:7).

‡ Jesus Christ is holy, born without sin in His bloodline, for His Father was God Almighty. He would become the only Perfect Sacrifice to take away our sins and remove its power and penalty from us.

§ The Greek word is translated, "relative." Many scholars believe Elizabeth was Mary's maternal aunt.

¶ This verse can be translated in two different ways. "There is nothing impossible with God." Or, "The word of God will never fail." The translator has chosen to include both for this verse.

** As translated from the Aramaic text.

†† Implied in the context.

To have the mother of my Lord* come and visit me?
⁴⁴The moment you came in the door and greeted me,
My baby danced inside me with ecstatic joy!
⁴⁵Great favor is upon you, for you have believed
Every word spoken to you from the Lord!"

Mary's Prophetic Song

⁴⁶And Mary sang this song,

My soul is ecstatic, overflowing with praises to God!
⁴⁷My spirit bursts with joy over my Life-Giving-God!
⁴⁸For He set His tender gaze upon me, His lowly servant girl.†
And from here on, everyone will know
That I have been favored and blessed!
⁴⁹The Mighty One has worked a mighty miracle for me;
Holy is His name!
⁵⁰Mercy kisses all His godly lovers,
From one generation to the next!‡
⁵¹Mighty power flows from Him
To scatter all those who walk in pride!
⁵²Powerful princes He tears from their thrones
And He lifts up the lowly to take their place!§
⁵³Those who hunger for Him will always be filled,¶
But the smug and self-satisfied, He will send away empty!
⁵⁴Because He can never forget to show mercy,
He has helped His chosen servant, Israel,
⁵⁵Keeping His promises to Abraham**
And to his descendants forever!"

⁵⁶Before going home, Mary stayed with Elizabeth for about three months.††

---

* An obvious prophetic revelation was given to Elizabeth from the Holy Spirit about what had happened with Mary.
† The Aramaic text is, "He set His gaze upon the willingness of His mother."
‡ Mary is quoting Psalm 103:17.
§ Implied in the text.
¶ Mary is quoting Psalm 107:9.
** Mary understood by revelation that the Christ child would fulfill the promises of mercy that God gave to Abraham. See Genesis 22:16-18.
†† The cultural practice of the Hebrews was that during the first three months of pregnancy, the mother would do nothing but rest.

The Birth of the Prophet John

[57]When Elizabeth's pregnancy was full-term, she gave birth to a son. [58]All her family, friends, and neighbors heard about it, and they too were overjoyed, for they realized that the Lord had showered such wonderful mercy upon her! [59]And when the baby was eight days old, according to their custom, all the family and friends came together for the circumcision ceremony.* Everyone was convinced that they would name the baby, Zechariah, after his father. [60]But Elizabeth spoke up and said, "No, he has to be named John!"

[61]"What?" they exclaimed, "No one in your family line has that name!"

[62]So they gestured to the baby's father to ask what to name the child. [63]After motioning for a writing tablet, to the amazement of all, he wrote: "His name is John!"†

[64]Instantly Zechariah could speak again! And his first words were praise to the Lord! [65]Then the fear of God fell on the people of their village and the news of this astounding event traveled throughout the hill country of Judea. Everyone was in awe over it! [66]All who heard this news were astonished and wondered, "If a miracle brought his birth,‡ what on earth will this child become? Clearly, God's presence is upon this child in a powerful way!"

Zechariah's Prophecy

[67]Then Zechariah was filled to overflowing with the Holy Spirit and began to prophesy, saying,

[68]"Praise be to the exalted Lord, God of Israel,
For He has seen us through eyes of grace,
And comes as our Hero-God to set us free!
[69]He appears to us as a Mighty Savior
A Trumpet of Redemption§
From the house of David, His servant,
[70]Just as He promised long ago
By the words of His holy prophets.

---

* This ceremony was an important time of celebration in Jewish culture, for another child was born under the covenant of God with Israel. See Genesis 17:4-14 and Leviticus 12:1-3.
† The name *John* means "God's gift," or "God is gracious."
‡ Implied in the text.
§ Literal translation of the Aramaic. The Hebrew is "a horn of salvation."

⁷¹They prophesied He would come one day and save us
From every one of our enemies and from
The power of those who hate us!*
⁷²Now He has shown us
The mercy promised to our ancestors,
For He has remembered His holy covenant.†
⁷³⁻⁷⁵He has rescued us from the power of our enemies!
This fulfills the sacred oath He made with our father, Abraham!
Now we can boldly worship‡ God with holy lives,
Living in purity as priests§ in His presence every day!
⁷⁶And to you I prophesy, my little son,
You will be known as the prophet of the Glorious God!
For you will be a forerunner going before
The face of the Master
To prepare hearts to embrace the ways of God!¶
⁷⁷You will preach to His people the revelation of salvation-life,
The cancellation of our sins, to bring us back to God!**
⁷⁸The splendor-light of heaven's glorious Sunrise††
Is about to break upon us in holy visitation,
All because the mercy of our God is so very tender.
⁷⁹The Manifestation from heaven will come to us‡‡
With dazzling light to shine upon those
Who live in darkness, near death's dark shadow,§§
And He will illuminate the path that leads to the way of peace!"

⁸⁰Afterwards, their son grew up and was strengthened by the Holy Spirit and he grew in his love for God. John chose to live in the lonely wilderness until the day came when he was to be displayed publicly to Israel.

---

* Zechariah is quoting from Psalm 106:10.
† See Genesis 12:1-3. There is amazing Hebrew poetry contained in this passage. The names of John, Zechariah, and Elizabeth are all found in this verse. "He has shown His mercy" is the name John. "He has remembered," is the name Zechariah. "His holy covenant," is the name Elizabeth.
‡ Or, "serve."
§ The word for purity is a Hebrew homonym for "priesthood."
¶ Zechariah quotes from Malachi 3:1. This "Sunrise" is the appearing of Christ, the Messiah.
** Implied in the text.
†† Some believe this is a quote from Malachi 4:2.
‡‡ As translated from the Aramaic.
§§ Zechariah is quoting from Isaiah 9:2 and Isaiah 59:8.

Luke 2

The Birth of Jesus

¹⁻²During those days, the Roman Emperor, Caesar Augustus,* ordered that the first census be taken throughout his empire. (Quirinius was the governor of Syria at that time.) ³Everyone had to travel to their hometown to complete the mandatory census. ⁴⁻⁵So Joseph and his fiancé, Mary, left Nazareth,† a village in Galilee, and journeyed to their hometown in Judea, to the village of Bethlehem,‡ King David's ancient home. They were required to register there, since they were both direct descendants of David. Mary was pregnant and nearly ready to give birth.

⁶⁻⁷When they arrived in Bethlehem, Mary went into labor. Since there was no room in the inn, and with no proper place to give birth, Mary and Joseph went to a stable, and there she gave birth to her firstborn son. Wrapping the newborn baby in strips of cloth, they laid him in a feeding trough.

An Angelic Encounter

⁸That very night in a field near Bethlehem§ there were shepherds watching over their flock. ⁹Suddenly, an angel of the Lord appeared in radiant splendor before them, lighting up the field with the blazing glory of God, and the shepherds were terrified! ¹⁰But the angel reassured them, saying, "Don't be afraid. For I have come to bring you the good news, the most joyous news the world has ever heard! And it is for everyone,

---

* It is so ironic that the Roman emperors viewed themselves as "gods" while the little baby born in a feeding trough was the True God incarnate.

† "Nazareth" is taken from a Hebrew word for "branch" (Isaiah 11:1).

‡ The distance from Nazareth to Bethlehem is about sixty-five miles and it would have taken a number of days for them to arrive. Bethlehem means, "house of bread," the prophesied birthplace of Messiah. God controls all events, proven by the prophecy that Jesus would be born in Bethlehem, even though His parents were living in Nazareth. See Micah 5:2.

§ Many scholars believe that these were the fields where sacrificial flocks were kept for temple worship. How fitting that these shepherds would hear the announcement of the birth of the Lamb of God. Others believe these fields could have been near the field of Boaz, or even the very field where David once watched over the flocks of his father, Jesse.

everywhere! ¹¹For today in Bethlehem* a Rescuer was born for you! He is the Anointed Messiah, the LORD JEHOVAH!† ¹²You will recognize Him by this miracle sign—you will find a baby wrapped in strips of cloth and lying in a feeding trough!"

¹³Then all at once, a vast number of glorious angels appeared—the very armies of heaven! And they all were praising God, singing,

> ¹⁴"Glory to God in the highest realms of heaven!
> And a good hope to the sons of men!"

¹⁵When the choir of angels disappeared back to heaven, the shepherds said to each other, "Let's go! Let's hurry and find this Manifestation‡ that is born in Bethlehem and see for ourselves what the Lord has revealed to us!" ¹⁶So they ran into the village and found their way to Mary and Joseph. And there was the Baby lying in a feeding trough!

¹⁷Upon seeing this miraculous sign, the shepherds recounted what had just happened to them! ¹⁸Everyone who heard the shepherd's story was amazed, astonished by what they were told!

¹⁹But Mary treasured all these things in her heart and often pondered them. ²⁰The shepherds returned to their flock, ecstatic over what had happened. They were praising God and glorifying Him for all they had heard and seen for themselves, just like the angel had said!

Baby Jesus Presented in the Temple

²¹On the day of the baby's circumcision ceremony, eight days after His birth, they gave Him the name, Jesus, the name prophesied by the angel before He was born! ²²Then, after Mary's days of purification had ended, it was time for her to come with a sacrifice to the temple according to the laws of Moses after the birth of a son.§ So Mary and Joseph took baby Jesus to Jerusalem to be dedicated before the Lord. ²³For it is required in the law of the Lord,

"Every firstborn male¶ shall be one set apart for God!"

---

* The Greek text says, "the city of David."
† Translated literally from the Aramaic text. This is one of the most amazing statements found in the gospels declaring the deity of Jesus Christ.
‡ As translated from the Aramaic text. Or, "He is the Lord Yahweh, the Messiah."
§ This comes from Leviticus 12:1-7. When a son was born, the mother went through a forty day period of purification, and then she was to offer a sacrifice to complete the process.
¶ Exodus 13:2,12.

²⁴And, to offer a prescribed sacrifice,

> "Either a pair of turtle-doves or two young pigeons."*

²⁵As they came to the temple to fulfill this requirement, there was an elderly† man already there waiting; his name was Simeon, a resident of Jerusalem. He was a very good man, a lover of God who kept himself pure, and the Spirit of Holiness rested upon him! Simeon believed that the appearing was imminent of One called, The Refreshing of Israel.‡ ²⁶For the Holy Spirit had revealed to him that he would not see death before he saw the Messiah, the Anointed One of God! ²⁷This is why he had been moved by the Holy Spirit to be in the temple court at the very moment Jesus' parents entered to fulfill the requirement of the sacrifice! ²⁸So Simeon cradled the baby in his arms and began to praise God and prophesy, saying,

> ²⁹⁻³¹ "Lord and Master, I am Your loving servant,
> And now I can die content,
> For Your promise to me has been fulfilled!
> And with my own eyes I have seen Your Manifestation,§
> The Savior You sent into the world!
> ³² He will be Glory for Your people Israel,
> And the Revelation-Light
> For all people everywhere!" ¶

³³Mary and Joseph just stood there awestruck over what was being said about their baby! Then Simeon turned and blessed them and prophesied over Mary, saying,

> ³⁴⁻³⁵ "A painful sword** will one day pierce your inner being,
> For Your child will be rejected by many in Israel.
> And the destiny of your child is this:

---

* Because Joseph and Mary were somewhat poor—not yet receiving the gifts brought by the wise men, they offered a pair of doves or pigeons instead of a lamb (Leviticus 12:8). Mary offered a "sin-offering," showing her need of a Savior. Jesus would one day be offered as her True Lamb.
† Implied in the context.
‡ This is a name for Jesus, the Messiah. It can also be translated, "The Encourager of Israel."
§ As translated from the Aramaic text.
¶ This is a fulfillment of many Old Testament prophesies, such as those found in Isaiah 9:2, 40:5, 42:6, 49:6, 51:4, 60:1-3.
** This is a unique Greek word used for *sword.* It is literally, "a broad sword."

> He will be laid down* as a miracle-sign
> For the downfall† and resurrection of many in Israel.
> Many will oppose this sign, but it will expose to all
> The innermost thoughts of their hearts before God!"

³⁶⁻³⁷And there was also on that day in the temple court, a prophetess named Anna. She was from the Jewish tribe of Asher and the daughter of Phanuel.‡ Anna was an aged widow who had only been married seven years before her husband passed away. After he died, she chose to worship God in the temple continually. So for the last eighty-four years,§ she had been serving God night and day with prayer and fasting.

³⁸While Simeon was prophesying over Mary and Joseph and the baby, Anna walked up to them at that very moment and burst forth with a great chorus of praise to God for the child, Jesus! And from that day forward, she began telling everyone in Jerusalem who was waiting for their redemption, that the anticipated Messiah had come!¶

³⁹So when they had completed everything required of them by the law of Moses, Mary and Joseph and Jesus returned back to their home** in Nazareth in Galilee. ⁴⁰The child grew more powerful in grace, for He was being filled with wisdom; and the favor of God was upon Him.

* The Greek word translated "appointed" is actually, to "lie down." Jesus was laid in a tomb for us and rose again for us!
† The Greek word for "falling" can actually be translated, "downfall," or "destruction." Perhaps this is a prophecy of the cross of Jesus Christ, where many will rise or fall depending on what they do with Jesus' death and resurrection. We were all destined to be joined to Him in His death and resurrection (Galatians 2:20). Every believer experiences a "downfall" and a "resurrection."
‡ The name *Asher* means, "blessed." *Phanuel* means, "the face of God!"
§ Some Greek manuscripts make her age to be eighty-four. But the most reliable Greek and Aramaic texts state that she had been in the temple for eighty-four years! One scholar believed her actual age at that time to be 106. God is faithful to those who wait in faith! Both Simeon and Anna were privileged to touch the Christ before they died in faith!
¶ The Greek text literally says that Anna was telling everyone "who was looking for the redemption of Jerusalem." This is a figure of speech for the One who would come and set them free, i.e. the Messiah. What amazing prophetic words came through Simeon and Anna!
** Luke omits their journey to Egypt to spare Jesus from the death decree of Herod. That information is given to us by Matthew. But none of the Gospels give all the details of this period. Luke also writes nothing about the visit of the wise men (Matt. 2:1–12), and Matthew tells nothing of the shepherds and of Simeon and Anna (Luke 2:8–28). All four Gospels supplement each other. There was likely a large period of time that transpired between v. 38 and v. 39.

At Age Twelve, Jesus Visits the Temple

[41]Every year Jesus' parents went to worship at Jerusalem during the Passover Festival. [42]So when Jesus turned twelve, His parents took Him to Jerusalem as it was their custom to observe the Passover. [43]As they began their journey home, Joseph and Mary became aware that they had left Jesus behind in Jerusalem! [44]They had assumed He was somewhere in their entourage, and traveled on for a day before realizing Jesus was nowhere to be found! After a frantic search among relatives and friends, Jesus turned up missing! [45]When they couldn't find Him, Mary and Joseph returned to Jerusalem to make their search for Him.

[46]After being separated from them for three days, they finally found Him in the temple, sitting among the Jewish teachers*, both listening and asking questions of them. [47]All who heard Jesus speak were astounded at His intelligent understanding of all that was being discussed and at His wise, comprehensive answers to their questions! [48]His parents were shocked to find Him there and Mary scolded Him saying, "Son, don't You know Your father and I have been worried sick over not finding You? Why would You do this to us? We have searched for You everywhere!"

[49]Jesus said to them, *"Why would you need to search for me? Didn't you know that it was necessary for Me to be here in My Father's House, consumed with Him?"*[†]

[50]Yet Mary and Joseph didn't fully understand what Jesus meant. [51]Jesus went with them back home to Nazareth and was obedient to them. His mother[‡] treasured Jesus' words deeply in her heart. [52]As Jesus grew, so did His wisdom and maturity. The favor of men increased upon His life, for He was loved greatly by God.[§]

---

* Or, "rabbi's."

† The first recorded words of Jesus, when He was only twelve, are given to us here.

‡ Mary was an amazing woman and should be honored as the mother of our Lord Jesus Christ. She was the only human being that was with Jesus all the way from His birth to His death. She is also mentioned in Acts 1:14.

§ We know virtually nothing about the remaining eighteen years between this incident in Luke 2 and Luke 3 when Jesus goes to the Jordan to be baptized by the Prophet John. We know He grew in favor with God and men. He did so while serving His earthly father in a carpenter's shop. Every task we have can be an opportunity to grow in favor with God and men. It is likely that Joseph, Jesus' earthly father, died during this season of His life. This left Jesus with the responsibility as firstborn to provide for His family. Amazing mysteries surround this One who is too marvelous for words!

Luke 3

The Ministry of the Prophet John

¹⁻²Then all at once, a powerful prophetic message from God came to John, Zechariah's son, when he was living out in the lonely wilderness!* This prophetic commission came to John during the fifteenth year of the reign of Emperor Tiberius Caesar. Pontius Pilate was governor over Judea at that time, and Herod governor over Galilee, Herod's brother, Philip, was over the region of Ituraea and Trachonitis, and Lysanias was over Abilene,† and it happened during the days of the high priests, Annas and Caiaphas.‡

³So John went preaching and baptizing throughout the Jordan valley. He persuaded people to turn away from their sins and turn to God§ for the freedom of forgiveness. ⁴This was to fulfill what was written in the book of the Prophet Isaiah:

"Listen! You will hear a thunderous voice in the lonely wilderness telling you to wake up and prepare your hearts for the coming of the LORD JEHOVAH.¶ Every twisted thing in your lives must be made straight! ⁵⁻⁶Every dark way must be brought to the light! Wrongs righted! Injustices removed! Every heart of pride will be humbled low before

---

* Many believe that John was a member of the Qumran community of Jewish Essenes, who lived in the wilderness because they viewed the Jewish religious system as corrupt.

† A region west of Ituraea.

‡ As the forerunner of Jesus Christ, the emergence of the Prophet John was truly a hinge of human history, forever changing the world. Luke carefully dates this event by giving us no fewer than six markers. Historians are able to date the reign of Tiberius Caesar beginning in AD 14. His fifteenth year of reigning would be AD 28-29. Regarding Annas and Caiaphas, never in Jewish history had there been two high priests. The priesthood was corrupt, for even though Caiaphas, Annas' son-in-law, was the High Priest, it was Annas who remained the real authoritative leader behind the scenes (John 18:13, Acts 4:6).

§ This is actually the definition of repentance, which has two concepts. One is turning away from sin and the other, turning to God for freedom. They are linked together as one word, "repentance."

¶ Translated from the Aramaic.

Him. Every deception will be exposed and replaced by the truth* so that everyone everywhere will be ready to see the Life of God!"†

⁷And so John kept preaching to the many crowds who came out to be baptized, "You are nothing but the offspring of poisonous snakes—full of deception! Have you been warned to repent before the coming wrath of God? ⁸Then turn away from your sins, turn to God, and prove it by a changed life! Don't think for a moment that it's enough to simply be the favored descendants of Abraham; that's not enough to save you!‡ I'm telling you, God could make Abraham more sons out of stones if He chose to! ⁹Even now God's axe of judgment is poised to chop down your barren tree right down to its roots! And every tree that does not produce good fruit will be leveled and thrown into the fire!"

¹⁰The crowd kept asking him, "What then are we supposed to do?"

¹¹John told them, "Give food to the hungry, clothe the poor, bless the needy!"§

¹²Even the despised tax collectors came to John to be baptized, and they asked him, "What are we to do to prove our hearts have changed?"

¹³"Be honest," he replied. "Don't demand more taxes than what you are required to collect!"¶

¹⁴"And us?" asked some soldiers,** "What about us?"

John answered them, "Be content with what you earn. Never extort money, or terrify others by threats of violence or be guilty of accusing the innocent!"

¹⁵During those days, everyone was expecting the Messiah to come at any time, and many began to wonder if John might be the Christ.

---

* The Greek text, quoting from Isaiah 40:3-5, is most literally translated: "Wake up and make lines for the Lord, make His side-alleys straight. Every ravine will be filled, every mountain and hill shall be leveled, crooked straightened, rough ways smoothed, and all flesh shall see the salvation of God." Every honest scholar recognizes this as more than a road construction project, but implies a spiritual renewal in hearts.

† Translated from the Aramaic; the word for "life" often refers to salvation.

‡ Implied in the context. God values reformation over ritual.

§ The Greek text is literally, "The one with two tunics is to share with him who has none, and he who has food is to do likewise."

¶ True repentance is tied to actions, a change of heart and deeds, not just words.

** Or, "those serving as soldiers." They were likely temple police.

¹⁶But John made it clear by telling them, "There is One coming who is Supreme* and mightier than I! In fact, I'm not worthy of even being His slave!† I can only baptize you in this river, but He will baptize you into the Spirit of Holiness and into His raging fire!"‡ ¹⁷He has in His hands the authority to judge your heart and the power to sift and cleanse you! He will separate the valuable within you from that which is worthless.§ The valuable He will store up for use in His kingdom, but He will burn the worthless in a fire that no one can ever put out!"

The Arrest of John

¹⁸John used many similar warnings as he preached the good news and prepared⁹ the people. ¹⁹He even publicly rebuked Herod, the governor of Galilee, for the many wicked things he had done. He fearlessly reprimanded him for seducing and marrying his sister-in-law, Herodias. ²⁰And adding to his many other sins, Herod had John seized and locked up in prison.

The Baptism of Jesus

²¹⁻²²Then one day Jesus came to be baptized** along with all the others. As He was consumed with the spirit of prayer, all at once above Him the heavenly realm opened, and the Holy Spirit descended from heaven in the visible, tangible form of a dove†† and landed upon

---

* The word *supreme* is found in only the Aramaic text. John was a true prophet who pointed others to the Supreme One. There had not been a prophet in Israel for four hundred years until John came on the scene.

† Or, "loose his sandal strap," which was what only a slave would do.

‡ The Aramaic text reads, "He will baptize you into the Spirit of the Holy One and in Light." A baptism of light or fire would cleanse and change the person's life, giving new power to live for God and deal with every issue that hinders love and passion from burning in our hearts. It is the baptism of the Holy Spirit that is needed today.

§ The text is literally, "a winnowing fork is in His hand." This was a small pitchfork that was used to separate the chaff from the grain.

¶ Translated from the Aramaic text.

** Jesus identified with sinners, even at His baptism. Although He had no sin, He chose to become one with sinners and was washed by John as a preview of what would come when He became sin and was judged for our sins at the cross.

†† The dove, as an emblem of the Holy Spirit, was released by Noah from the ark. The final dove released never returned. Flying over the patriarchs and prophets, there was no one found upon whom He could land and rest. Not until Jesus, the Lamb of God! What a beautiful picture of a Dove resting upon a Lamb. To have the power of the Spirit (the dove), you need to have the nature of the Lamb (Jesus).

Him! Then God's audible voice was heard saying, *"My Son! You are my Beloved One!"* * *Through You I am fulfilled!"*†

The Ancestry of Jesus Christ

²³⁻³⁸Jesus, assumed to be "Joseph's son," was about thirty years old when He began His ministry.‡ Now here are the names of Mary's§ ancestors, from her father down, traced all the way back to Adam:

Eli,⁹ Matthat, Levi, Melki, Jannai, Joseph, Mattathias, Amos, Nahum, Esli, Naggai, Maath, Mattathias, Semein, Josech, Joda,

Joanan, Rhesa, Zerubbabel, Shealtiel, Neri, Melchi, Addi, Cosam, Elmadam, Er, Joshua, Eliezer, Jorim, Matthat, Levi, Simeon, Judah, Joseph, Jonam, Eliakim, Melea, Menna, Mattatha, Nathan, David,

Jesse, Obed, Boaz, Salmon, Nahshon, Amminadab, Admin, Arni, Hezron, Perez, Judah, Jacob, Isaac, Abraham, Terah, Nahor, Serug, Reu, Peleg, Eber, Shelah, Kenan, Arphaxad, Shem, Noah, Lamech, Methuselah, Enoch, Jared, Mahalaleel, Cainan, Enos, Seth, and Adam, who was the son of God.

(handwritten margin note: Lineage of Christ to Adam)

---

* The heavenly voice confirms the identity of Jesus as Messiah. God is quoting Psalm 2:7 and Isaiah 42:1, which are both considered as speaking of the Christ. God is publicly saying that Jesus is the long awaited and much loved Son, the Christ! The Trinity is clearly seen in this passage—Jesus, the Holy Spirit, and the Father.

† As translated from the Aramaic text. The Greek text states, "in whom I am greatly pleased." We hear the voice of the Father as the presence of the Holy Spirit comes upon the Son of God. What a beautiful picture of the triune God—Three-in-One.

‡ Old Testament priests could not begin their ministry until they were thirty years old. The number thirty is the biblical number of maturity. Both Joseph and David were promoted to the place of honor when they were thirty.

§ Scholars recognize that Matthew gives us the genealogy of Jesus from Joseph's family, while Luke's genealogy is from Mary's side, for Luke is the one gospel writer that gives much attention to women. Neither Matthew nor Luke gives a complete genealogy.

¶ Many believe this was the father of Mary.

Luke 4

The Wilderness Temptations of Jesus

¹⁻²From the moment of His baptism, Jesus was overflowing with the Holy Spirit! He was taken by the Spirit from the Jordan into the lonely wilderness of Judea,[*] to experience the ordeal of testing[†] by the accuser for forty days.[‡] He ate no food during this time and ended His forty day fast very hungry. ³It was then the Devil said to Him, "If you are really the Son of God just command this stone to turn into a loaf of bread for You!"

⁴But Jesus replied, "I will not![§] For it is written in the Scriptures,[¶] *"Your life does not come only from eating bread but from God!"* ^{**}

⁵Suddenly the Devil lifted Jesus up high into the sky^{††} and in a flash showed Him all the kingdoms and regions of the world. ⁶⁻⁷The devil said to Jesus, "All of this—with all its power, authority, and splendor—is mine to give to whomever I wish. Just do one thing, and You will have it all! Simply bow down to worship me and it is Yours! You will possess it all!"

⁸But Jesus replied to him, *"I will not! For it is written in the Scriptures, "Only One is worthy of your adoration! You will bow in worship before the Lord your God and love Him supremely!"* ^{‡‡}

---

* The Holy Spirit's leading is not always into comfort and ease. The Spirit may lead you, as He did Jesus, into places where we are proven, tested, and strengthened for our future ministry. After the greatest affirmation from heaven, came the greatest time of testing for our Lord.
† The Greek word used here means, "to test with a sinister motive."
‡ Jesus' baptism and then forty days of wilderness temptations evoke the historical narrative of the Hebrew exodus through the Red Sea and the forty years of wilderness testing.
§ Jesus refused to turn stones to bread, but today He transforms the "stony" hearts of men and converts them into living bread to give to the nations.
¶ Jesus, the Living Word is quoting the written Word from Deuteronomy 8:3. If the Living Word used the written Word against the Enemy's temptations, how much more do we need the revelation of what has been written so we can stand against all his snares?
** This is implied by both the Greek and Aramaic texts. In Matthew's parallel account of this verse and in the Aramaic text it adds: "and by every revelation from the mouth of God."
†† Implied, for the Greek text simply says, "took Him up" without telling us where.
‡‡ This is taken from Deuteronomy 6:13 & 10:20.

⁹Next, the Devil took Jesus to Jerusalem and set Him on the highest point of the temple and tempted Him, saying, "If You really are the Son of God, jump down in front of all the people! You'll not be hurt! ¹⁰⁻¹¹For isn't it written in the Scriptures, 'God has given His angels instructions to protect You from harm? For the hands of angels will hold You up and keep You from hurting even one of Your feet on a stone. They will come if You jump!'" *

¹²Jesus replied to him, *"But it is also written in the Scriptures, 'How dare you provoke the Lord your God!'"* †

¹³That finished the Devil's harassment for the time being, so he stood off at a distance, retreating until the right time came to return and tempt Jesus again.

Jesus' Ministry of Power Begins

¹⁴Then Jesus, overflowing with the Holy Spirit's power, returned to Galilee just as His fame began to spread throughout the region. He taught in the meeting places‡ and He offered everyone glory!§

¹⁵⁻¹⁷When He came to Nazareth, where He had been raised, He went into the meeting house as He always did on the Sabbath day. Jesus came to the front to read the Scriptures⁹ so they handed Him the scroll of the Prophet Isaiah. He unrolled the scroll and began to read where it is written,

¹⁸⁻¹⁹*"The Spirit of the Lord is upon me, and He has anointed Me to be Hope for the poor, Pardon for prisoners,** Freedom for the brokenhearted, and New Eyes for the blind. I have come to share the message of Jubilee,†† for the time of God's great acceptance‡‡ has arrived!"* §§

---

* This is implied in the text. The devil is quoting from Psalm 91:11-12, but he misapplies it.
† Jesus was not deceived and quotes here from Deuteronomy 6:16.
‡ This was the Jewish synagogue, the meeting place for the Jewish people. Every small village which had at least ten families would erect a meeting house where they would come and hear visiting teachers expound the Scriptures.
§ As literally translated from the Aramaic text.
¶ It was the custom to read the Scriptures in Hebrew and then paraphrase them into Aramaic, the common language of that day.
** It is literally, "prisoners of war."
†† Implied in the text. The Isaiah passage is associated with the proclamation of the Year of Jubilee. See Leviticus 25:8-17; Isaiah 58:6 and 61:1-2.
‡‡ Or, "favor." This can be translated, "the years when God will accept man."
§§ This is found in Isaiah 61:1.

[20]After He read this, He rolled up the scroll, handed it back to the
minister, and sat down. Everyone kept staring at Jesus wondering what
He was about to say! [21]Then He added, "*These Scriptures came true today in
front of you!*"

[22]Everyone was deeply impressed by how well Jesus spoke, and were
in awe of the beautiful words of grace that came from His lips. But
they were surprised at His presumption to speak as a prophet,* so
they said among themselves, "Who does He think He is? Isn't He
merely Joseph's son who grew up here in Nazareth?"†

[23]So Jesus said to them, "*I suppose you'll quote me the proverb, 'Doctor, go and
heal yourself before you try to heal others!' And you'll say, 'Work the miracles here in
your hometown that we heard you did in Capernaum!'* [24]*But let Me tell you, no prophet
is welcomed or honored in his own hometown!*

[25]"*Isn't it true that there were many widows in the land of Israel during the days of the
Prophet Elijah when he locked up the heavens for three and a half years, and brought a
devastating famine over all the land?* [26]*But he wasn't sent to any of the widows living
in that region. Instead, he was sent to a foreign place, to a widow in Zarephath of Sidon!*
‡ [27]*Or have you not considered that the prophet Elisha healed only Naaman,* § *the
Syrian, rather than one of the many Jewish lepers living in the land!*"

[28]When everyone present heard those words, they erupted with furious
rage!¶ [29]They mobbed Jesus and threw Him out of the city, dragging Him
right to the edge of the cliff on the hill on which the city had been built,
ready to hurl Him off! [30]But Jesus supernaturally walked right through
the crowd, leaving them all stunned!**

Jesus Confronts a Demonized Man

[31]Then Jesus went to Capernaum in Galilee and began to teach the
people on the Sabbath day. [32]His teaching astounded them, for He spoke
with penetrating words that manifested great authority! [33]But in the

* Implied in the context.

† Implied in the text. Jesus' true Father was not Joseph, but Yahweh.

‡ *Zarephath* means, "the place of refining." *Sidon* means, "fishery" and was a Phoenician seaport city.

§ Both the Aramaic and Greek texts have, "Naaman, the Aramean" or descendant of Aram. The Arameans inhabited current day Syria. *Naaman* means, "pleasantness."

¶ They got the point of Jesus' sermon—jubilee had come, not only for them but for those they hated. This infuriated them to the point of wanting to kill Jesus.

** Implied in the text. The Greek text clearly implies a supernatural event.

congregation, there was a demonized man who screamed out with a loud voice, ³⁴"Hey You! Go away and leave us alone! I know who You are! You're Jesus of Nazareth, God's Holy One! Why are You coming to meddle with us? You have come to destroy us already!"*

³⁵Just then the demon hurled the man down on the floor in front of them all, but Jesus rebuked the demon, saying, *"Shut up and come out of him!"* And the demon came out of him without causing the man any harm.

³⁶Great amazement swept over the people as they said among themselves, "What kind of Man is this who has such power and authority? With a mere word He commands demons to come out and they obey Him!" ³⁷And the reports about Jesus began to spread like wildfire throughout every community in the surrounding region.

Jesus Heals Many

³⁸Leaving the meeting that day, Jesus went into Simon's house, where Simon's mother-in-law was sick with a very high fever. They begged Jesus to help her. ³⁹Jesus stood over her, rebuked the fever, and she was healed instantly! Then she got up and began to serve them!

⁴⁰At sunset,† the people brought all those who were sick to Jesus to be healed. Jesus laid His hands on them one by one and they were all healed of different ailments and sicknesses. ⁴¹Demons also came out of many of them! The demons knew that Jesus was the Anointed Messiah and would shout while coming out, "You are the Son of God!" But Jesus would rebuke them and command them to be silent.

⁴²At daybreak the next morning, all the crowds came and searched everywhere for Him, but Jesus had already left to go to a secluded place. They finally found Him and held Him tightly, begging Him to stay with them in Capernaum. ⁴³But Jesus said, *"Don't you know there are other places I must go so I can offer to them the hope of God's kingdom-realm? This is what I have been sent to do."* ⁴⁴So Jesus continued to travel and preach in the Jewish meeting places throughout the land.

---

* This is not a question, but an assertive statement.

† People came before dark, for that was when the Sabbath began. The Sabbath was to be a day of rest for every Jew. It began at sunset on Friday and ended at sunset on Saturday.

Luke 5

Jesus Selects Disciples

¹On one occasion, Jesus was preaching to the crowds on the shore of the Sea of Galilee.* There was a vast multitude of people pushing to get close to Jesus to hear the Word of God. ²He noticed two fishing boats nearby at the water's edge with the fishermen nearby rinsing their nets. ³Jesus climbed into the boat belonging to Simon Peter and asked him, *"Let Me use your boat. Push it off a short distance away from the shore so I can speak to the crowds."* ⁴Then Jesus sat down and began to teach the people from the boat. When He had finished, He said to Simon Peter, *"Now let's go out into the deep to cast your nets and you will have a great catch!"*

⁵"But Master," Peter replied, "we've just come back from fishing all night and didn't catch a thing, but if You insist, we'll go out again and let down our nets because of Your word!" ⁶When they pulled up their nets, they were shocked to see such a huge catch of fish—so much that their nets were ready to burst! ⁷So they waved to their business partners in the other boat for help. They ended up completely filling both boats with fish until their boats began to sink!†

⁸When Simon Peter saw this miracle,‡ he knelt down at Jesus' feet and begged Him, saying, "Go away from me, Master, for I am nothing but a sinful man!" ⁹⁻¹⁰Simon Peter and the fishermen, including his fishing partners, James and John, the sons of Zebedee, were totally awestruck over the miracle catch of fish.

---

* Or, "Gennesaret," which is known as the Sea of Galilee.
† It has been estimated that this was a catch of nearly one ton of fish, normally what is caught in two weeks. The miracle is even greater when considered that fishing was normally only done at night.
‡ Implied in the text.

Then Jesus answered Peter saying, *"Don't yield to your fear, Simon Peter. From now on you will catch men for salvation!"** ¹¹After pulling their boats to the shore, they just left everything behind and followed Jesus!

Jesus, the Healer

¹²One day while Jesus was ministering in a certain city, He came upon a man covered with leprous sores. When the man realized it was Jesus, he fell on his face at Jesus' feet and begged to be healed, saying, "If You are only willing, You could completely heal me!"

¹³⁻¹⁴Then Jesus reached out and touched him† and said to him, *"Of course I am willing to heal you, and now you will be healed!"* Instantly the leprous sores were healed and his skin smooth! Jesus said, *"Tell no one what has happened, but go now to the priest and show him you've been healed; and to show you are purified, make an offering for your cleansing just as Moses commanded. You will become a living testimony to them!"*

¹⁵After this miracle, the news about Jesus spread even farther! Massive crowds continually gathered to hear Him speak and to be healed from their illnesses. ¹⁶But Jesus would often slip away from them and go into the lonely wilderness to pray.

¹⁷One day many Jewish religious leaders, known as "separated ones,"‡ along with experts of Moses' law came from every village of Galilee, throughout Judea, and even from Jerusalem to hear Jesus teach. And the power of the Lord God was surging through Him to instantly heal the sick! ¹⁸Just then some men came carrying a paraplegic man on a stretcher and were attempting to bring him in—past the crowd—to set him down in front of Jesus. ¹⁹But because there were so many people crowding the door, they had no way to bring him inside. So they crawled onto the roof, dug their way through the roof tiles, and lowered the man down, stretcher and all, into the middle of the crowd right in front of Jesus! ²⁰Seeing this demonstration of their faith, Jesus said to the paraplegic man, *"My friend, your sins are forgiven!"*

---

* Translated literally from the Aramaic text.
† For the religious Jew, to touch a leper was forbidden because of the contamination. Jesus was not defiled in touching the leper; the leper was healed!
‡ Literally, "Pharisees" which means, "separated ones."

²¹The Jewish religious leaders and the experts of the law* immediately began to make objections among themselves, "Who does this man think He is to speak such blasphemy? Only God alone can forgive sins!"

²²⁻²³Jesus knew their very thoughts and answered them, *"Why do you argue in your hearts over what I do and think that it is blasphemy for Me to say his sins are forgiven? Let Me ask you, which is easier to prove? When I say, 'Your sins are forgiven' or when I say, 'Stand up, carry your stretcher and walk?'"* Then Jesus turned to the paraplegic man and said, ²⁴*"To prove to you that I, the Son of Man,† have the authority on earth to forgive sins, I say to you now, Stand up! Carry your stretcher and go on home, for you are healed!"*

²⁵Then, in an instant, the man rose before their eyes! He stood up, picked up his stretcher and went home—giving God all the glory every step he took! ²⁶The people were seized with astonishment and dumbfounded over what they had just witnessed! And they all were praising God, remarking over and over in their amazement, "Incredible! What an extraordinary miracle we've seen today!"

Jesus Calls Matthew to Follow Him

²⁷Afterwards, Jesus went out and looked for a man named Matthew‡ and found him sitting at his tax booth, for he was a tax collector. Jesus simply said to him, *"Be My disciple and follow Me!"* ²⁸And from that moment on, Matthew got up, left everything behind, and followed Him!

²⁹⁻³⁰Matthew invited Jesus to his home for dinner along with many tax collectors and other notable sinners, for Matthew wanted to throw a banquet to honor Jesus. While they were all sitting together at the table, the Jewish religious leaders and experts of the law began to complain to Jesus' disciples saying, "Why would you defile yourselves by eating and drinking with tax collectors and sinners? Doesn't Jesus know it's wrong to do that?"§

³¹But Jesus overheard their complaining and spoke up and said, *"Who goes to the doctor for a cure? Those who are well or those who are sick?¶* ³²I have

---

* Or "scribes."

† The "Son of Man" was a commonly used term by the Jewish teachers for the Messiah.

‡ The Greek text is, "Levi," which was another name for Matthew.

§ Implied in the text.

¶ The word used here is the Greek word for "evil." Sickness is a form of evil in God's eyes. Jesus came to heal the "evil" or the sicknesses of earth.

not come to call the 'righteous,' but to call those who fail to measure up, and bring them to repentance!"

A Question About Fasting

[33]But Jesus' critics questioned Him, "John the Prophet is well known for leading his disciples to frequently fast and pray. As the religious leaders of the land, we do the same. Why then do You and all Your disciples spend most of your time feasting at banquets?"*

[34]Jesus replied, "*Should you make the sons of the bridal chamber fast while celebrating with the Bridegroom?* [35]*But soon, when the Bridegroom is taken away from them, then you will see them fasting!*"

[36]And, He gave them this illustration: "*No one rips up a new garment to make patches for an old, worn out one. If you tear up the new to make a patch for the old, it will not match the old garment!* [37]*And who pours new wine into an old wineskin? If someone did, you know what would happen. The old wineskin would burst and the new wine would be lost.* [38]*New wine must always be poured into new wineskins.* [39]*Yet you say, 'The old ways are better,' and you refuse to even taste the new that I bring!*"

---

* It is likely that Matthew held his banquet on one of the Jewish fast days.

Luke 6

Jesus is Lord of the Sabbath

¹One Sabbath day, Jesus and His disciples happened to be walking through a field of ripe wheat. His disciples plucked some heads of grain and rubbed the husks off with their hands and ate it. ²This infuriated some of the Jewish religious leaders. So they said to Jesus, "Why are You allowing Your disciples to harvest grain on the Sabbath day? Don't you know it's not permissible according to the Law?"

³Jesus replied, *"Haven't you read the Scriptures? Haven't you read what King David did when he was hungry?* ⁴*He entered the sanctuary of God and took the bread of God's presence right off the sacred table, and shared it with his men.***It was only lawful for the priests to eat the bread of God's presence!* ⁵*You need to know that the Son of Man is no slave to the Sabbath day. I am Master over the Sabbath!"*

⁶⁻⁷On another Sabbath day, Jesus was teaching in the Jewish meeting house. In the room there was a man with a deformed right hand. Everyone was watching Jesus closely, especially the Jewish religious leaders and experts of the law who were anxious to see if He would heal on a Sabbath day, for they were eager to find a reason to accuse Him of breaking the Jewish laws. ⁸But Jesus, knowing their every thought, said to the man, *"Come and stand here in the middle of the room."* So the man got up and came forward.

⁹Jesus said to all who were there, *"Let me ask you a question. Which is better, to heal or to do harm on the Sabbath day? I have come to save a life, but you have come to find a life to destroy!"*

¹⁰One by one Jesus looked into the eyes of each person in the room, and then said to the man with the deformed hand, *"Stretch out your arm and open your hand!"* With everyone watching intently, he stretched out his arm and his hand was immediately healed! ¹¹The room erupted

---

* This incident is found in 1 Samuel 21:1-6.

31

with bitter rage because of this Sabbath day healing; and from that moment on, they plotted among themselves about how they might harm Jesus!

Jesus Chooses Twelve Apostles

¹²Shortly afterwards, Jesus went up into the high hills to spend the whole night in prayer to God.* ¹³At daybreak He called together all of His followers and selected from among them twelve and appointed them His "apostles."†

¹⁴⁻¹⁶Here are their names: Simon, whom He named Peter, and Andrew, Peter's brother, James, and John, and Philip, and Bartholomew,‡ and Matthew, and Thomas, and James who was the son of Alphaeus, and Simon, known as a fiery political zealot, and Judah who was the son of James,§ and Judas the locksmith,¶ the one who later betrayed Jesus.

Jesus Ministers to a Massive Crowd

¹⁷Jesus and His apostles came down from the hillside to a level field where a large number of His disciples were waiting, along with a massive crowd of people who had gathered from all over Judea, Jerusalem, and the coastal district of Tyre and Sidon. ¹⁸They had all come to listen to the Manifestation, so that they could be healed of their diseases** and be set free from the demonic powers that tormented them. ¹⁹The entire crowd eagerly tried to come near Jesus and to just touch Him to be healed because supernatural power kept emanating from Him, healing all who came!

---

* This was the pattern of Jesus in the Gospel accounts before He would make great decisions or before great events in His life. He sought the Father, He saw what the Father wanted, and then Jesus simply obeyed as the Perfect Son.

† An *apostle* means "an ambassador," "missionary," or a "sent-one." The apostles were all different in their personalities and came from different backgrounds. Similarly, Jesus chooses many today who don't all look, act, or sound alike.

‡ Many scholars believe that Bartholomew was Nathaniel, mentioned in John 1:45-46.

§ He is also called, "Thaddeus" as mentioned in Matthew 10:3 and Mark 3:18.

¶ The name *Judas* is actually Judah. "Iscariot" is not his last name or the name of a town. It is taken from a Hebrew word that means "lock"—Judah the "locksmith." He most likely was the one who locked the collection bag, which means he had the key and could pilfer the funds at will. It is his sad history that he wanted to lock up Jesus and control Him for his own ends.

** This is the literal translation of the Aramaic text.

Jesus Taught Them What Matters Most

²⁰Then looking intently at His followers, Jesus began His sermon, *"Happy are you when you are poor, for you will experience the reality of the kingdom-realm!*

²¹*"Happy are you when you are consumed with hunger and desire, for that's when you will be completely satisfied!*

"Happy are you when you weep in complete brokenness, *for that's when you will laugh with unrestrained joy!*

²²*"Happy are you when you are hated, excommunicated, slandered, and your name spoken of as 'evil' because of your love for Me, the Son of Man!* ²³*I promise you, that as you experience these things you will celebrate and dance with overflowing joy! And the heavenly reward of your faith will be abundant, because you are being treated the same way as your forefathers, the prophets!*

²⁴*"But what sorrows await those of you who are rich in this life only! For you've already received all the comfort you'll ever get!*

²⁵*"What sorrows await those of you who are complete and content with yourselves! For hunger and emptiness is coming to you!*

"What sorrows await those of you who laugh now, having received all your joy in this life only! For grief and wailing is coming to you!

²⁶*"What sorrows await those of you who are always honored and lauded by others! For that's how your forefathers treated every other false prophet!*

Love Your Enemies

²⁷*"But if you will listen, I say to you, love your enemies and do something wonderful†️ for them well in return for their hatred. When someone curses you, bless them in return!* ²⁸*When you are mistreated and harassed by others,‡ accept it as your mission to pray for them!* ²⁹*And to those who despise you, continue to serve them and minister to them still!§ And if someone takes away your coat, give him as a gift your shirt as well!* ³⁰*When someone comes to beg from you, give to them what you have! When things are wrongly taken from you, do not demand they give it back!* ³¹*And however you wish to be treated by others, this is how you should treat everyone else!*

---

* Implied in the text.

† As translated from the Aramaic text.

‡ The Greek text implies a witchcraft curse.

§ As literally translated from the Aramaic text. The Greek text states, "If someone strikes you on one side of your jaw, allow him to strike you on the other side."

[32]"Are you really showing true love by only loving those who love you back? Even those that don't know God will do that! [33]Are you really showing compassion when you only do good deeds to those who do good deeds to you? Even those who don't know God will do that!

[34]"And if you lend money only to those you know will repay you, what credit is that to your character? Even those who don't know God do that! [35]But love your enemies and continue to treat them well. When you lend money, don't despair if you are never paid back, for it is not lost! You will receive a rich reward and you will be known as true children of the Most High God, having His same nature! For Your Father is famous for His kindness to heal* even the thankless and cruel! [36]Have compassion for others, just as Your heavenly Father overflows with compassion for all."

Judging Others

[37]Jesus said further, "Forsake the habit of criticizing and judging others, and then you will not be criticized and judged in return! Don't look at others and pronounce them, 'Guilty!' and you will not experience guilty accusations! Forgive over and over and you will be forgiven over and over! [38]Give generously and generous gifts will be given back to you, shaken down to make room for more! Abundant gifts will pour out upon you with such an overflowing measure that it will run over the top! Your measurement of generosity becomes the measurement of your return!"

[39]Jesus also quoted these proverbs: "What happens when a blind man pretends to guide another blind man? They both stumble into a ditch! [40]And how could the apprentice know more than his master, for only after he is fully qualified will he be at that level. [41]Why do you focus on the flaw in someone else's life and fail to notice the glaring flaws of your own life? [42]How could you say to your friend, 'Here, let me show you where you're wrong,' when you are guilty of even more than he is? You are overly critical, splitting hairs and being a hypocrite! First you must acknowledge your own "blind spots" and deal with them before you will be able to deal with the "blind spot" of your friend!

The Fruit of Your Life

[43]"You'll never find choice fruit hanging on a bad, unhealthy tree. And rotten fruit doesn't hang on a good, healthy tree! [44]Every tree will be revealed by the quality of fruit that it produces. Figs or grapes will never be picked off thorn trees. [45]People are known in this same way! Out of the virtue stored in their hearts, good and upright people will produce good fruit. But out of the evil hidden in their hearts, evil ones will produce what

---

* Literal translation of the Aramaic text.

is evil. For the overflow of what has been stored in your heart will be seen by your fruit and will be heard in your words!

⁴⁶"What good does it do for you to say I am Your Lord and Master, and yet whatever I teach you is not put into practice? ⁴⁷Let Me describe the one who truly follows Me and does what I say. ⁴⁸He is like a man that chooses the right place to build a house and then lays a deep and secure foundation. And when the storms and floods rage against that house, it continues to stand strong and unshaken through the tempest, for it has been wisely built on the right foundation. ⁴⁹But the one who has heard My teaching and does not obey it is like a man who builds a house without laying any foundation whatsoever. When the storms and floods rage against that house, it will immediately collapse and become a total loss! So which of these two builders will you be?" *

---

* This last question is an important summary implied in the context.

Luke 7

Jesus Heals With Merely a Word

¹After Jesus finished giving revelation* to the people on the hillside, He went on to Capernaum.† ²⁻³There lived a Roman military captain who had a beloved servant that he valued highly who was sick and at the point of death. When the captain heard that Jesus was in the city, he sent some respected Jewish elders to plead with Him to come and heal his dying servant. ⁴So they came to Jesus and told Him, "The Roman captain is a wonderful man and if anyone deserves to have a visit from You, it is him! Won't You please come to his home and heal his servant? ⁵For he loves the Jewish people and he even built our meeting hall for us."

⁶⁻⁷So Jesus started off with them, but on His way there, He was stopped by friends of the captain and was given this message, "Master, don't bother to come to me in person, for I am not good enough for you to enter my home. I'm not worthy enough to even come out to meet One like You, but if You would just release the manifestation of healing right where You are, I know that my young servant will be healed! ⁸But, unlike You,‡ I am just an ordinary man, yet I understand the power of authority and I see that authority operating through You.§ I have soldiers under me who I simply command and they obey my every word. And I also have authorities over me that I likewise obey. So, Master, just speak the word and healing will flow!"

⁹Jesus marveled at this! He turned around and said to the crowd that had followed Him, *"Listen everyone! Never have I found— even one among the people of God—a man like this who believes so strongly in Me!"* ¹⁰Jesus then spoke the healing word from a distance!¶ When the man's friends returned to the home, they found the servant completely healed and doing fine!

---

* Or "teaching." The Greek word used here is *rhema*.
† This is literally, "the hamlet of Nahum," the village where Nahum the prophet lived.
‡ The text implies that the Roman captain acknowledged that Jesus was more than a man.
§ Implied in the text.
¶ Implicit in the miracle was that Jesus released the word of healing for the servant!

Jesus Raises the Dead

¹¹Shortly afterwards Jesus left on a journey for the village of Nain with a massive crowd of people following Him along with His disciples. ¹²As He approached the village, He met a multitude of people in a funeral procession who were mourning as they were carrying the body of a young man to the cemetery. The boy was his mother's only son, and she was a widow. ¹³When the Lord saw the grieving mother, His heart broke for her and with great tenderness He said to her, *"Please don't cry."* ¹⁴Then He stepped up to the coffin and touched it as the pallbearers came to a halt. Jesus spoke to the corpse and said, *"Young man, I say to you, arise and live!"*

¹⁵Immediately, the young man moved, sat up, and began to talk to those nearby! Jesus presented the son back to his mother, alive! ¹⁶A tremendous sense of holy mystery swept over the crowd as they witnessed this miracle of resurrection![*] And the next moment they all began to shout with great praises to God saying, "God Himself has visited us to bless His people! A Great Prophet has now appeared among us!" ¹⁷The news of Jesus and this miracle raced throughout Judea and the entire surrounding region!

The Prophet John's Question

¹⁸Afterwards John's disciples reported to him in prison[†] about all the wonderful miracles and the works Jesus was doing. ¹⁹So John dispatched two of his disciples to go and inquire of Jesus. ²⁰When they came before the Master, they asked Him, "Are You the coming Messiah we've been expecting or are we to continue to look for someone else? John the Prophet has sent us to You to seek Your answer." ²¹Without answering[‡] Jesus turned to the crowd and immediately began to heal many of their incurable diseases as His miracle power freed many from their suffering! He restored the gift of sight to the blind, and He drove out demon spirits from those who were tormented! ²²Only then did Jesus answer the question posed by John's disciples. *"Now go back and tell John what you have just seen and heard here today. The blind are now seeing! The crippled are now walking! Those who were lepers are now cured; those who were deaf are now hearing, those who*

---

* Implied in the text.
† Implied in the context. See also Luke 3:20 and Matthew 11:2-19.
‡ Or, "at that time."

were dead ones are now raised back to life and the poor and broken* are given the hope of salvation!† ²³And tell John these words: 'The blessing of heaven comes upon those who never lose their faith‡ in Me—no matter what happens!'"

²⁴After John's messengers departed, Jesus began to speak about John before the audience crowded around Him, saying, "What kind of man did you expect to see out in the wilderness? Did you expect to see a man who would be easily influenced and shaken by the shifting opinions of others? ²⁵Who did you really go there to see? Did you expect to see a man decked out in the splendid fashion of the day?§ They are the ones that live in the lap of luxury, embracing the values of this world. ²⁶Or did you discover a true prophet out in the lonely wilderness? Yes, John was a legitimate prophet, even more than that! ²⁷He was the fulfillment of this Scripture:

'See, I am sending my prophetic messenger¶
Who will go ahead of Me
And prepare hearts to receive Me!' **

²⁸"Throughout history there was never found a man as great as John the Baptizer. Yet those who now walk in God's kingdom -realm, though they appear to be insignificant, they will become even greater than he!"

²⁹When the common and disreputable people among the audience heard Jesus say this, they acknowledged that it was the truth, for they had already experienced John's baptism. ³⁰But the hearts of the Jewish religious leaders and experts of the law rejected the clear purpose of God by refusing to be baptized by John!

³¹Jesus continued, saying, "How could I describe the people of this generation? Can't you see? ³²You're just like children playing games on the playground, complaining to friends— 'You don't like it when we want to play Wedding! And you don't like it when we want to play Funeral! Why is it you will neither dance nor mourn? ††

³³"So, when the Prophet John came fasting and refused to drink wine, you said, 'He's crazy! There's a demon in him!' ³⁴Yet when the Son of Man came and went to feasts

---

* This fulfills many Old Testament references to the coming of the Messiah, including Isaiah 29:18-19; 35:5- 6; and 61:1.
† Jesus is assuring John that His message brings life and salvation, not judgment and wrath.
‡ The Greek text is literally, "Blessed are those who are not offended over Me."
§ See Matthew 3:4.
¶ Or, "angel."
** This is quoted from Malachi 3:1.
†† Implied in the context.

and drank wine, you said, 'Look at this man! He is nothing but a gluttonous pig and a drunkard! He spends all His time with tax collectors and other notorious sinners!'

³⁵"Nevertheless I say to you, the wisdom of God* will be proven true by the expressions of godliness in everyone who follows Me!"

A Woman Kisses Jesus' Feet

³⁶Afterwards one of the Jewish religious leaders named Simon† asked Jesus to his home for dinner. Jesus accepted the invitation and went to Simon's home and took His place at the table. ³⁷In the neighborhood there was an immoral woman of the streets, known to all as a prostitute, who heard about Jesus being in Simon's house. Taking with her an exquisite flask made from alabaster,‡ filled with the most expensive perfume, she went right into the home of the Jewish religious leader, and knelt down at the feet of Jesus in front of all the guests! ³⁸Broken and weeping, she covered His feet with tears that fell from her face! She kept crying and drying off His feet with her long hair. Over and over she kissed Jesus' feet, and then she opened her flask and anointed His feet with her costly perfume as an act of worship!

³⁹When Simon the Jewish religious leader saw what was happening, he thought to himself, "This man can't be a true prophet! If He were really a prophet He would know what kind of sinful woman is touching Him!"

⁴⁰Jesus spoke up and said, *"Simon, I have a word for you."*

"Go ahead, Teacher, I want to hear it," he answered.

⁴¹*"It's a story about two men who were deeply in debt. One owed the bank $100,000* § *and the other only owed $10,000. ⁴²When it was obvious that neither of them would be able to repay their debts, the kind banker very graciously wrote off the debt and forgave them all that they owed. Tell me, Simon— which of the two debtors would be the most thankful? Which one would love the banker most?"*

⁴³Simon answered, "I suppose it would be the one with the greatest debt forgiven."

---

* Or more literally, "wisdom is vindicated by all her children."
† The name *Simon* is supplied from verse 40.
‡ This is a soft, cream colored stone often used for jars and vases.
§ The Greek text uses the monetary term, "denarius." The picture of the story is that one owed over a year's wages, the other much less.

"*You're right,*" Jesus agreed. [44]Then He spoke to Simon about the woman still weeping at His feet, "*Don't you see this woman kneeling here? She is doing for Me what you didn't bother to do. When I entered your home as your guest, you didn't think about offering Me water to wash the dust off My feet. Yet she came into your home and washed My feet with her many tears, and then she dried My feet with her hair.* [45]*You didn't even welcome Me into your home with the customary kiss of greeting, but from the moment I came in, she has not stopped kissing My feet.* [46]*You didn't take the time to anoint my head and feet with fragrant oil, but she anointed My feet with the finest perfume.* [47]*She has been forgiven of all her many sins. This is why she has shown Me such extravagant love. But the one who assumes they have very little to be forgiven will love me very little.*"

[48]Then Jesus said to the woman at His feet, "*Your sins are all forgiven!*" [49]But all the dinner guests began to say among themselves, "Who is the One who can even forgive sins?" [50]Then Jesus said to the woman, "*Your faith in Me has given you life! Now you may leave and walk in the ways of peace!*"

Luke 8

Jesus Ministers throughout the Land

¹Soon afterwards Jesus began a ministry tour throughout the country visiting cities and villages to announce the fantastic news of God's kingdom-realm! His twelve disciples travelled with Him ²and also a number of women who had been healed of many illnesses under His ministry and set free from demonic power. Jesus had cast out seven demons from one woman. Her name was Mary Magdalene, for she was from the village of Magdala.* Among them was Susanna and ³Joanna, the wife of Chusa, who managed King Herod's household.† Many other women who supported Jesus' ministry from their own personal finances also travelled with Him.‡

The Mysteries of God's Kingdom-Realm

⁴Massive crowds gathered from many towns to hear Jesus as He taught them using metaphors and parables,§ such as this: ⁵*"A farmer went out to sow seeds for a harvest. As He scattered His seed some of it fell on the hard pathway and was quickly trampled down and unable to grow and became nothing but bird seed! ⁶Some fell upon the gravel and though it sprouted, it couldn't take root; it withered for lack of moisture. ⁷Other seed fell where there was nothing but weeds. It too was unable to grow to full maturity for it was choked out by the weeds. ⁸Yet some of the seed fell into good, fertile soil, and it grew and grew and flourished until it produced more than a hundredfold harvest, a bumper crop!"*

---

* Implied by the word *Magdalene*. The ancient village of Magdala has only recently been discovered near the current town of Migdol.

† Some scholars believe that Chusa was the government official mentioned in John 4:46-53.

‡ To travel with a rabbi was considered a high honor. Yet it was not permitted in the culture and time of Jesus' ministry for a woman to be mentored by a rabbi. Jesus elevates women into a place of honor and respect, in spite of the cultural limitations. It was these wealthy women who provided for Jesus' care. Luke is the one gospel writer who brings out the many times Jesus honored women.

§ Jesus' preferred teaching method was through the story of a parable (Matthew 13:34). It required the listener to be humble, teachable, and open to truth. Revelation from God can be found through the doorway of an allegory.

Then Jesus added, shouting out to all who would hear—"*Listen with your heart and you will understand!*"

[9]Later His disciples came to Jesus to ask Him privately what deeper meaning was found in this parable. [10]He said, "*You have been given a teachable heart, perceiving the divine mysteries of God's kingdom. But to those who don't have a listening heart, My words are merely stories. For even though they have eyes, they are blind to see its true meaning,* and even though they listen, they won't receive its full revelation.*

[11]"*Here then, is the deeper meaning to my parable: The Manifestation[†] of God is the seed that is sown into hearts. [12]The hard pathway represents the hard hearts of men who hear the Word of God, but 'the slanderer'[‡] quickly snatches away what was sown in their hearts to keep them from believing and experiencing salvation. [13]The seed falling upon the gravel represents those who initially respond to the Manifestation with joy, but soon afterwards, when a season of temptation and difficulty comes to them, they wither and fall away, for they have no root in the truth and their faith is temporary.[§] [14]The seed which falls into the weeds represents the hearts of those who will hear the Manifestation of God, but its growth is quickly choked off by their own anxious cares, the riches of this world, and the fleeting pleasures of this life. This is why they never become mature and fruitful. [15]But the seed which fell into good, fertile soil represents those lovers of truth who hear it deep within their hearts. They respond by clinging to the Word, keeping it dear as they endure all things in faith. This is the seed that will one day bear much fruit in their lives!*

The Revelation-Light

[16]"*No one lights a lamp and then hides it, covering it over or putting it where its light won't be seen. No, they place the lamp on a lampstand where others are able to benefit from its brightness! [17]Because this revelation-lamp now shines within you, nothing will be hidden from you— it will all be revealed. Every secret of the kingdom[§] will be unveiled and out in the open, made known by the revelation-light! [18]So, pay careful attention to your hearts as you hear My teaching, for to those who have an open heart even more revelation until*

---

* This is taken from Isaiah 6:9-10. See also Jeremiah 5:21 and Ezekiel 12:2.
† From the literal Aramaic text. The Greek word, *logos* can also be translated, "Manifestation."
‡ Or, "the Devil." The Greek word, *diabolos* means, "the slanderer."
§ From the Aramaic text.
¶ Implied in the context of Jesus teaching on the mysteries of God's kingdom (v.10).

it overflows will be given to them! And those who do not listen with an open heart, what little light they imagine they have—that too will be taken away."*

Jesus' True Family

[19]Then Mary, Jesus' mother, and her other sons[†] came to where Jesus was teaching, but they couldn't get through the crowd that had gathered around Him. [20]He was told, "Your mother and brothers[‡] are standing outside wanting to speak with you." [21]But Jesus told them, *"These who come to listen to Me are like My mothers and My brothers! They're the ones who long to hear and to put God's Word into practice!"*

Peace in the Storm

[22-23]One day Jesus said to His disciples, *"Let's get in a boat and go across to the other side of the lake."* So they set sail, but Jesus soon fell asleep as the wind began to rise. The fierce wind became a violent squall that threatened to swamp their boat! [24]So they woke Him up, saying, "Master, Master, we're sinking! Don't you care that we're going to drown?" Jesus woke up and with great authority rebuked the howling wind and surging waves and instantly they stopped and became as smooth as glass! [25]Then Jesus said to them, *"Why are you fearful? Have you lost your faith in Me?"*[§] Shocked and shaken, they said with amazement to one another, "Who is this Man [¶] who has authority over winds and waves and they obey Him?"

A Demonized Man Set Free

[26-29]As soon as they stepped ashore on the other side of the lake in the land of the Gerasenes, they were confronted by a demon possessed madman from a nearby town. Many times he had been kept under guard and bound with chains, but repeatedly the many demons inside him would throw him into convulsions, breaking his shackles and driving him out of the town into the countryside. He had been demonized for

---

* This verse contains a complicated ellipsis, which is a literary function of omitting certain information to invite discovery. The ellipsis of the text has been supplied by making explicit what is implicit in the context. The parables of the sower and of the lamp are similar, in that they speak of the heart that receives truth. The manifestation of the kingdom is a "seed" that grows within us and a "lamp" that glows within us.

† These were the half-brothers/sisters of Jesus. Mary had other sons and daughters. Jesus' Father was not Joseph, but the Father of Eternity. See also Mark 6:3.

‡ See John 7:5.

§ Implied in the text.

¶ The answer to that question is found in Jeremiah 31:35. He is the Lord of Hosts!

a long time and was living naked in a cemetery among the tombs! But when he saw Jesus, he fell at His feet and screamed out, "What are You doing here? You are Jesus, the Son of the Most High God!" Jesus then commanded the demons to come out of him as they shouted out, "We beg You; don't torture us!"

³⁰Jesus spoke to the man and said, *"What is your name?"*

"Mob" the demons answered, "We're a mob,* for there are many of us here in this man! ³¹We beg you; don't banish us to the bottomless pit of the abyss!"†

³²On the hillside nearby there was a very large herd of pigs, so the demons pled with Jesus, "Let us enter into the pigs." ³³So Jesus ordered the mob of demons to come out of the man and enter the pigs! The crazed herd of swine stampeded over the cliff into the lake and all of them were drowned!

³⁴When those who were tending the pigs saw what had happened, they ran off in fear and reported it to the nearby town and throughout the countryside. ³⁵Then the people of the region came out to see for themselves what had happened. And when they came to where Jesus was, they discovered the notorious‡ madman totally set free! He was clothed, speaking intelligently, and sitting at the feet of Jesus. They were shocked! ³⁶Eyewitnesses to the miracle reported all that they had seen and how the demonized man was completely delivered from his torment.

After hearing about such amazing power, the townspeople became frightened! ³⁷Soon, all the people of the region of the Gerasenes and the surrounding country begged Jesus to leave them, for they were gripped with fear! So Jesus got into the boat, intending to return to the Galilee. ³⁸But the man who had been set free, begged Jesus over and over not to leave, saying "Let me be with You!" Yet Jesus sent him away with these instructions, ³⁹*"Return to your home and your family and tell them all the wonderful things God has done for you!"* So the man went away and preached about the amazing miracle Jesus worked in his life to everyone who would listen.

---

* The Greek word used for "mob" is literally, "legion," which was the largest unit of the Roman military and represented up to 6800 soldiers.
† See Revelation 9:1 and 20:1-3. The "abyss" is the place of imprisonment for Satan and his demons.
‡ Implied in the context.

More Miracles of Healing

⁴⁰When Jesus returned to Galilee, the crowds were overjoyed for they had been waiting for Him to arrive. ⁴¹⁻⁴²Just then, a man named Jairus, the leader of the local Jewish congregation, fell before Jesus' feet. He desperately begged Him to come and heal his twelve year old daughter, his only child, because she was at the point of death. Jesus started to go with him to his home to see her, but a very large crowd now surrounded Him. ⁴³In the crowd that day was a woman who had suffered greatly for twelve years from slow bleeding. Even though she had spent all that she had on "healers,"* she was still suffering. ⁴⁴Pressing in through the crowd, she came up behind Jesus and touched the tassel† of His prayer shawl. Instantly her bleeding stopped and she was healed!

⁴⁵Jesus suddenly stopped and said to His disciples, *"Someone touched Me! Who is it?"*‡

While they all denied it, Peter pointed out, "Master, everyone is touching You, trying to get close to You! The crowds are so thick§ we can't walk through all these people without being jostled!"

⁴⁶Jesus replied, *"Yes, but I felt power surge through me! Someone touched me to be healed, and they received their healing!"*

⁴⁷When the woman realized she couldn't hide any longer, she came and fell trembling at Jesus' feet! Before the entire crowd she declared, "I came to touch You, Jesus, for I knew if I could just touch even the fringe of Your robe, I would be healed!"

⁴⁸Jesus responded, *"Beloved daughter, your faith in Me has healed you! You may go with My peace!"*

⁴⁹While Jesus was still speaking to the woman, someone came from Jairus' house to inform him, "There's no need to bother the Master any further. Your daughter has passed away. She's gone."

---

* Translated from the Aramaic text, which states literally, "the house of healers." This phrase is not found in many Greek texts.
† This was on the corner of the prayer shawl and the tassel was said to symbolize all the commandments and promises of God. The woman was laying hold of a promise for healing.
‡ Jesus already knew the answer to His question; He wanted the woman to come forward and acknowledge her healing.
§ There were many crowds around Jesus, the Living Word. And there are many today who crowd around the Bible, the written Word. But only those who "touch" the Scriptures in faith receive its promises, just like the sick woman received her healing.

⁵⁰When Jesus heard this He spoke up, *"Jairus, don't yield to your fear! Just be filled with faith in Me and she will live again!"* ⁵¹So when they arrived at the house, Jesus only allowed Peter, John, and James—along with the child's parents to go inside. ⁵²Jesus told those left outside who were sobbing and wailing with grief, *"Stop crying; she is not dead, she's just asleep and must be awakened!"* ⁵³But they laughed at Him,* knowing for certain that she had died! ⁵⁴Jesus approached the body, took her by her hand, and called out with a loud voice, *"My sleeping child, awake! Rise up!"* ⁵⁵⁻⁵⁶Instantly her spirit returned to her body and she stood up! Jesus directed her stunned parents to give her something to eat and ordered them not to tell anyone what just happened.

---

* They did not realize that Jesus was using "sleep" as a metaphor for death.

Luke 9

Jesus Sends Out His Apostles

[1]Jesus summoned together His twelve apostles* and imparted to them authority over demons and the power to heal every disease. [2]Then He commissioned them to preach the kingdom-realm of God and to instantly heal the sick to demonstrate that the kingdom had arrived. And as He sent them out, He gave them these instructions, [3]*"Take nothing extra on your journey.† Just go as you are! Don't carry a staff, a backpack, food, money, not even a change of clothes!* [4]Whatever home welcomes you as a guest, remain there and make it your base of ministry. [5]And wherever your ministry is rejected and not welcomed, you are to leave that town and shake the dust off your shoes‡ as a sign that you will not be held responsible for their fate."* [6]So the apostles departed and went into the villages with the wonderful news of God's kingdom-realm and they healed diseases wherever they went!

Herod's Perplexity

[7]Now Herod, the governor, was confused and perplexed when he began to hear the reports of all the miracles of Jesus. Many were saying, "John the Baptizer has come back to life again!" [8]Others were saying, "This has to be Elijah who has reappeared or one of the prophets of old who has risen from the dead!" These were the rumors circulating throughout the land. Herod exclaimed, [9]"Who is this man? I keep hearing about Him over and over! It can't be the Prophet John; I had him beheaded!"§ Herod was very eager to meet Jesus.

---

* As translated from certain Greek manuscripts and implied in the context.

† Why did Jesus tell them to go empty-handed? To trust and walk in faith. But also, because the five items they were told not to bring, they already possessed in their spiritual counterparts that are found in Him (i.e. He is our Treasure, our Strength, our Living Bread, our Provider, and our Righteousness).

‡ More than a metaphor this was an actual custom of the day to signify that you would not be responsible for their fate.

§ See Mark 6:14-29.

Jesus Feeds Thousands

¹⁰When the apostles returned from their ministry tour, they told Jesus all the wonders and miracles they had witnessed. Jesus, wanting to be alone with the Twelve, quietly slipped away with them toward Bethsaida.* ¹¹But the crowds soon found out about it and took off after Him! When they caught up with Jesus, He graciously welcomed them all and began to teach them more about the kingdom of God and healed any who were sick.

¹²As the day wore on, the Twelve came to Jesus and told Him, "It's getting late. You should send the crowds away to the surrounding villages and farms to get something to eat and find shelter for the night. There's nothing to eat here in the middle of nowhere."

¹³Jesus responded by saying, *"You have the food to feed them."*† They replied, "All we have are these five small loaves of bread and two dried fish. Do you really expect us to go and buy food for all these people? ¹⁴There are nearly 5,000 men here plus women and children!"‡

Then He told His disciples, *"Have them all sit down in groups of fifty each."* ¹⁵⁻¹⁶After everyone was seated, Jesus took the five loaves and two fish, and looking up into heaven He gave thanks for the food. Then in the presence of His disciples, He broke off pieces of bread and fish, and kept on giving more to each disciple to give to the crowd! It was multiplying§ before their eyes! ¹⁷Everyone ate until they were filled, and afterwards they gathered up the leftovers—it came to exactly twelve baskets full!

Jesus Prophesies His Death and Resurrection

¹⁸One time when Jesus was praying in a quiet place with His disciples nearby, He came over to them and asked, *"Who do people really think I am?"*

¹⁹They answered, "Some are convinced You're the Prophet John who has returned; yet others say You are Elijah, or perhaps one of the Jewish prophets brought back from the dead."

²⁰Then Jesus asked them, *"But who do you believe that I am?"* Peter spoke up, "You are the Anointed One, God's Messiah!"

---

* *Bethsaida* means, "house of fishing."
† In the Greek text, the word *you* is emphatic. Jesus tells His disciples that they have food to give to others. It is true, because He lives within us; we can give others the living bread, and if need be, multiply food for others to eat. We are to focus on what we have, not what we don't have!
‡ Implied in the text.
§ This is supplied information, a summary statement of what happened, implied in the text.

²¹Then Jesus gave strict orders and warned them not to tell this to anyone yet, telling them, ²²*"The Son of Man is destined to experience great suffering and face complete rejection by the Jewish leaders and religious hierarchy.* He will be killed and raised back to life on the third day."*

What it Means to Follow Jesus

²³Then He said to all His followers, *"If you truly desire to be My disciple, you must disown your own life completely, embrace My cross† as your own, and surrender to My ways.‡* ²⁴*For if you choose self-sacrifice, giving up your lives for My glory, you will embark on a discovery of more and more of true life. But if you choose to keep your lives for yourselves, you will lose what you try to keep.* ²⁵*What's the point if you gain all the wealth and power of this world— everything it could offer you—and yet lose your own soul? Never!* ²⁶*Then why are you ashamed of being My disciple? Are you ashamed of the revelation-truth§ I give to you?*

"I, the Son of Man, will one day return in My radiant brightness, with the holy angels, and in the splendor and majesty of My Father, and I will be ashamed of all who are ashamed of Me. ²⁷*But I promise you this: There are some of you standing here right now who will not die until you have witnessed the presence and the power of the kingdom-realm of God!"* ¶

The True Glory of Jesus

²⁸Eight days later, Jesus took Peter, James, and John and climbed a high mountain to pray. ²⁹As He prayed, His face began to glow until it was a blinding glory streaming from Him. His entire body illuminated a radiant glory; so intense became His brightness** that it made His clothing blinding white, like flashes of lightning! ³⁰⁻³¹All at once two men suddenly appeared in glorious splendor; it was Moses and Elijah! They began to speak with Jesus about His soon departure†† from this

---

* The Greek text is literally, "the elders, chief priests and scribes." These three groups were represented in the "religious hierarchy" of the Sanhedrin, a council of seventy-one leaders.

† This could also mean being willing to suffer and die for Christ.

‡ Implied in the text.

§ The Greek word is *logos*.

¶ This was a prophecy of what was about to take place with Peter, James, and John on the mountain of transforming glory. This promise would be fulfilled as they experienced the power of the kingdom of God and the cloud of glory.

** Implied in the context of what was taking place. The Greek text says, "the appearance of His face was altered." The light shined through His clothing as His glorified body became brilliant with light. This is called Jesus' transfiguration.

†† The actual word in Greek is *exodus*.

world and the things He was destined to accomplish in Jerusalem. ³²Peter and his companions had become drowsy, but now fully awake, they saw the true glory and splendor of Jesus standing there and the two men with Him.

³³As Moses and Elijah were about to return into heaven, Peter impetuously blurted out— "Master, this is amazing to see the three of you together! Why don't we just stay here in the glory and set up three shelters—one for You, one for Moses, and one for Elijah!"

³⁴While Peter was still speaking, the radiant cloud of glory suddenly began to form above them and overshadowed them. As the glory cloud completely enveloped them, they were struck with fear! ³⁵Then the voice of God thundered from within the cloud, saying, *"This is My Son, My Beloved One!* Listen carefully to all He has to say!"*

³⁶And when the thunderous voice faded away and the cloud disappeared, standing there was Jesus alone! Peter, James and John were left speechless and awestruck. But they never mentioned a word to anyone about what they had seen!

The Power of Faith

³⁷The next day when they came down from the mountain, a massive crowd was waiting there to meet them. ³⁸And a man in the crowd shouted out desperately, "Please, Teacher, I beg of You, do something about my boy! He's my only child! ³⁹He's possessed by an evil spirit that makes him scream out in torment! This demon rarely leaves him and only after a long struggle! It throws him into convulsions and he foams at the mouth. And when it finally does leave him, he's left with horrible bruises! ⁴⁰I begged Your disciples to drive it out of him, but they didn't have enough power to do it!"

⁴¹Jesus responded, *"You are an unbelieving people with no faith! Your lives are twisted with lies that have turned you away from doing what is right! How much longer should I remain here offering you hope?"*† Then He said to the man, *"Bring your son to Me."*

⁴²But as the boy approached, the demon slammed him to the ground, throwing him into violent convulsions! Jesus sternly commanded the demon to come out of the boy and immediately it left! Then He instantly

---

* Several Greek manuscripts have "My Chosen One."
† As translated from Aramaic text.

healed the boy of his injuries and returned him to his father, saying,*
"*Here is your son.*" ⁴³Everyone was awestruck! They were all stunned,
seeing the power and majesty of God flow through Jesus! ⁴⁴And while
everyone marveled, trying to process what they had just witnessed,
Jesus turned to His disciples and said, "*This is very important, so listen
carefully and remember My words: The Son of Man is about to be betrayed and given
over to the authority of men.*" ⁴⁵But the disciples were unable to perceive
what He was saying for it was a veiled mystery to them, and they were
too embarrassed to ask Him to explain it.

True Greatness

⁴⁶Soon the disciples began to argue, and became preoccupied over who
would be the greatest one among them. ⁴⁷Fully aware of their innermost
thoughts, Jesus called forward a little child to His side and said to them,
⁴⁸"*If you tenderly care for this little child † on My behalf, you are tenderly caring for
Me. And if you care for Me, you are honoring My Father who sent Me. For the one who
is least important in your own eyes is actually the most important one of all.*"

⁴⁹The Disciple John spoke up and said, "Master, we found someone who
was casting out demons using Your name and we tried to stop him,
because he doesn't follow You like we do."

⁵⁰Jesus responded, "*You shouldn't have hindered him, for anyone who is not against
you is your friend.*"‡

Jesus' Journey to Jerusalem

⁵¹Jesus passionately determined to leave for Jerusalem and let nothing
distract Him from fulfilling§ His mission there, for the time for Him to
be lifted up was drawing near.¶ ⁵²So He sent messengers** ahead of Him as
envoys to a village of the Samaritans. ⁵³But as He approached the village,
they were turned away; they would not allow Him to enter for He was on

---

* Implied in the text.

† The little child becomes a representative of unimportant people in general. Treating the least
with care and respect makes us truly great.

‡ Jealousy blinds our hearts. Nine disciples combined could not cast out a demon spirit (v.40),
but they were jealous of this one who did.

§ Implied in the context.

¶ This refers to the cross where Jesus was "lifted up" upon a tree to bear the sins of all
mankind. His true exaltation into glory was through the sacrifice of His life upon Calvary's
cross. Nothing would turn Him aside from being our Sin-bearer and Redeemer.

** The most literal translation is, "He sent angels before His face."

His way* to worship in Jerusalem. ⁵⁴When the disciples, James and John, realized what was happening they came to Jesus and said, "Lord, if You wanted to, You could have commanded fire to fall down from heaven just like Elijah did† and destroyed all these wicked people."

⁵⁵But Jesus turned and rebuked them sharply, saying, *"Don't you realize what comes from your hearts when you say that? For the Son of Man did not come to destroy life, but to bring life to the earth!"‡* ⁵⁶And they went to another village instead.

The Cost to Follow Jesus

⁵⁷On their way, someone came up to Jesus and said, "I want to follow You wherever You go!"

⁵⁸Jesus replied, saying, *"Yes, but remember this: Even animals in the field have holes in the ground to sleep in and birds have their nests, but the Son of Man has no place here to lay down His head."*

⁵⁹Jesus turned to another and said, *"Come be My disciple!"*

But he replied, "Someday I will, Lord, but first let me fulfill my duty as a good son§ and wait until my father passes away."

⁶⁰Jesus told him, *"Don't wait for your father's burial. Let those who are already dead wait for death! But as for you, go and proclaim everywhere that God's kingdom-realm has manifested!"*

⁶¹Still another said to Him, "Lord, I want to follow You too! But first let me go home and say goodbye to my entire family."

⁶²Jesus responded by telling him, *"Why do you keep looking backwards to your past and have second thoughts about following Me? When you turn back you are useless to God's kingdom-realm!"*

---

* The Samaritans had their own place of worship on Mount Gerizim and they were hostile to Jews who wanted to worship in Jerusalem. There were many cultural, religious, and ethnic hostilities between Jews and Samaritans.

† This sentence is translated from the Aramaic. The earliest Greek manuscripts do not include, "just like Elijah did." Some Greek texts state, "Do you want us [the disciples] to call down fire and destroy them?"

‡ Translated from Aramaic. Most Greek manuscripts do not include the words of Jesus here.

§ The text is literally, "allow me first to go and bury my father." This is an idiom for waiting until his father passed away. He wanted an inheritance in this life as his security.

Luke 10

Jesus Commissions Other Disciples

¹After this, the Lord Jesus formed thirty-five teams among the other disciples. Each team was two disciples, seventy in all,* and commissioned them to go ahead of Him into every town He was about to visit. ²He released them with these instructions, *"The harvest is huge and ripe! But there are not enough harvesters to bring it all in! As you go, plead with the Owner of the Harvest to drive out† into His harvest fields many more workers! ³Now off you go! I am sending you out even though you feel vulnerable as lambs going into a pack of wolves! ⁴You won't need to take anything‡ with you— trust in God alone! And don't get distracted from My purpose by anyone you might meet along the way. ⁵Once you enter a house, speak to them and say, 'God's blessing of peace be upon this house!' ⁶If a lover of peace§ resides there, then your peace will rest upon that household! But if you are rejected, your blessing of peace will come back upon you. ⁷Don't feel the need to shift from one house to another, but stay put in one home during your time in that city. Eat and drink whatever they serve you. Receive their hospitality, for you are My harvester, and you deserve to be cared for.*

⁸*"When you enter into a new town, and you have been welcomed by its people, simply follow these rules: Eat¶ what is served you. ⁹Heal the sick, and tell them all, 'God's kingdom-realm has arrived and is now within your reach!' ¹⁰But when you enter a city and they do not receive you, say to them publicly, ¹¹'We wipe from our feet the very dust of your streets as a sign against you! Understand this: You have rejected God's offer of His kingdom-realm!'"*

---

* The text states they were "other" (i.e. other than the Twelve). A few Greek manuscripts have "seventy-two."

† This is the term used many times in the Gospels for driving out or casting out demons! The Lord of the Harvest must cast them forth!

‡ The text states literally, "take no money, no knapsack, no sandals." The implication is they were to trust in God alone for all their needs to be met.

§ Literally, "son of peace" which is a way of saying, "a godly man."

¶ This instruction to "eat what was served" was given twice, for the Jewish dietary laws were not meant to be a hindrance in their ministry nor were they to demand certain foods.

¹²Jesus continued, *"Let Me say it clearly. On the day of judgment, the wicked people of Sodom will have a lesser degree of judgment than the city that rejects you, for Sodom did not have the opportunity that was given to them!"**

Jesus Condemns the Unrepentant Cities

¹³*"How disastrous it will be for the city of Korazin! How horrible for the city of Bethsaida! For if the powerful miracles that I performed in Korazin and Bethsaida had been done in Tyre and Sidon, they would have humbled themselves and repented, and turned from their sins! ¹⁴Tyre and Sidon†* *will face a lesser degree of judgment than you will on the day of judgment! ¹⁵And Capernaum! Do you really think you'll be highly exalted because of the great things I have done there? No! You'll be brought down to the depths of hell because of your rejection of Me!*

¹⁶Jesus then concluded His instructions to the seventy with these words: *"Remember this: Whoever listens to your message is actually listening to Me! And anyone that rejects you is rejecting Me, and not only Me but the One who sent Me!"*

The Seventy Return

¹⁷When the seventy returned to Jesus, they were ecstatic with joy, telling Him, "Lord, even the demons obeyed our words when we commanded them in Your name!"

¹⁸To this Jesus replied, *"And while you were ministering I was watching Satan topple until he fell suddenly from heaven like lightning to the ground! ¹⁹Now you understand, I have imparted to you all my authority to trample over his kingdom. You will trample upon every demon before you and overcome every power‡ Satan possesses! Absolutely nothing will be able to harm you as you walk in this authority! ²⁰However, your real source of joy isn't merely that these spirits submit to your authority, but that your very names are written in the journals of heaven, and that you belong to God's kingdom! This is the true source of your authority!"§*

²¹Then Jesus, overflowing with the Holy Spirit's joy, exclaimed: *"Father, thank You, for You are Lord Supreme over heaven and earth! And the great revelation of this authority You have hidden from those who are proud, those wise in their own eyes, and You have shared it with these who have humbled themselves! Yes, Father— this is what pleases Your heart and the very way You've chosen to extend Your kingdom, to give*

---

* Implied in the context.

† Tyre and Sidon were two Gentile cities on the Mediterranean coast which were known for their wickedness.

‡ The Greek text is literally, "snakes and scorpions" which are emblems of demonic powers.

§ Implied in the text.

to those who become like trusting children! ²²"Father, You have entrusted Me with all that You are and all that You have. No one fully knows the Son except the Father. And No one fully knows the Father except the Son. But the Son is able to introduce and reveal the Father to anyone He chooses."

²³Later when Jesus was alone with the Twelve, He said to them, "You are very privileged to experience all these things! ²⁴Many kings and prophets of old would have given everything to see these days of miracles that you've been favored to see. They would have given everything to hear the revelation you've been favored to hear! Yet they didn't get to see as much as a glimpse or get to hear even a whisper."

Loving God, Loving Others

²⁵Just then a religious scholar stood before Jesus in order to test His doctrines. He posed this question, "Teacher, what requirement must I fulfill if I want to live forever in heaven?" ²⁶Jesus replied, "What does Moses teach us? What do you read in the Law?"

²⁷The religious scholar answered, "It states, 'You must love the Lord God with all your heart, all your passion, all your energy, and your every thought! And you must love your neighbor as well as you love yourself."

²⁸Jesus said, "That is correct; now go and do exactly that and you will live!"

²⁹But wanting to justify himself, he questioned Jesus further, saying, "What do You mean by 'my neighbor?'"

³⁰Jesus replied, "Listen and I will tell you. There was once a Jewish* man travelling from Jerusalem to Jericho when bandits robbed him along the way. They beat him severely, stripped him naked, and left him half dead.

³¹Soon, a Jewish priest walking down the same road came upon the wounded man. Seeing him from a distance, the priest crossed to the other side of the road and walked right past him, not turning to help him one bit.

³²Then later, a religious man, a Levite,† also came walking down the same road and likewise crossed to the other side to pass by the wounded man without stopping to help him.

---

* Although the text does not describe him as "Jewish," it is clearly implied in the context.
† The Levites were temple assistants, helping the priests. 1 Chronicles 23:28-32.

³³But finally another man, a despised Samaritan,* came upon the bleeding man and was moved with tender compassion for him. ³⁴He stooped down and gave him first aid, pouring olive oil on his wounds, disinfecting them with wine and bandaging them to stop the bleeding. Lifting him up, he placed him upon his own donkey and brought him to an inn. Then he took him from his donkey and carried him to a room for the night. ³⁵The next morning, he took out money from his own wallet and gave it to the innkeeper with these words, 'Take care of him until I come back from my journey. If it costs more than this, I will repay you when I return.' ³⁶Now tell Me, which one of the three men who saw the wounded man proved to be the true neighbor?"

³⁷The religious scholar, responded, "The one who demonstrated kindness and mercy."

Jesus said, *"You must go and do the same as he!"*

Jesus Visits Martha and Mary

³⁸⁻³⁹As Jesus and the disciples continued on their journey, they came to a village where a woman welcomed Jesus into her home. Her name was Martha and she had a sister named Mary. Mary soon sat down attentively before the Master, absorbing every revelation He shared. ⁴⁰Soon Martha became exasperated by the numerous household chores in preparing for her guests, so she interrupted Jesus and said, "Lord, don't You think it's unfair that my sister left me to do all the work by myself? You should tell her to get up and help me." ⁴¹

But the Lord answered her and said, *"Martha, My beloved Martha. Why are you upset and troubled, pulled away by all these distractions? Are they really that important? ⁴²Mary has discovered the one thing most important by choosing the most excellent place—to sit here at My feet. She is undistracted and I won't take this privilege from her."*

---

* There was racial tension in those days between Jews and Samaritans. Samaritans were considered half-breeds by the religious Jews. A Samaritan would be the most unlikely to stop and help a Jewish man.

Luke 11

Jesus Teaches About Prayer

¹One day as Jesus was in prayer, one of His disciples came over to Him as He finished and said, "Would you teach us a model prayer* that we can pray, just like John did for his disciples?"

²So Jesus taught them this prayer: *"Our Father-God, we worship You and honor Your sacred name. May Your Holy Spirit come upon us and cleanse us.†‡ Bring Your kingdom-realm to the earth.* ³*And keep giving us each day‡ what is needed for that day.* ⁴*Forgive our sins as we ourselves release forgiveness to those who have wronged us. And rescue us every time we face tribulations§."*

⁵Then Jesus gave this illustration: *"Imagine what would happen if you were to go to one of your friends in the middle of the night, and pound on his door and shout: 'Please! Do you have some food you can spare?* ⁶*A friend just arrived at my house unexpectedly and I have nothing to serve him!'¶* ⁷*But your friend says, 'Why are you bothering me? The door is locked and my family and I are all in bed! Do you expect me to get up and give you our food?'* ⁸*But listen—because of your shameless persistence, even though it's the middle of the night, your friend will get up out of his bed and give you all that you need.* ⁹⁻¹⁰*So it is with your prayers. If you will keep on asking, you'll receive! If you will keep on seeking, you'll discover! And if you will keep on knocking on heaven's door, it will one day open for you! Every persistent one will get what they ask for! Every persistent seeker will discover what they need! And everyone who knocks persistently will one day find an open door!*

¹¹*"Let me ask you this: Do you know of any father that would give his son a snake on a plate when he asked for a serving of fish instead?** Of course not!* ¹²*Do you know of any father that would give his daughter a spider when she had asked for an egg instead?*

---

* Implied in the text.
† Translated from some of the earliest Greek manuscripts.
‡ The text is literally, "Give us our needed bread for the coming day."
§ Or, "orderals."
¶ It was the culture of the day to honor every guest and provide a meal when they arrived.
** Some manuscripts substitute the word *fish* with *loaf* (bread) and the word *snake* with *a stone.*

Of course not! ¹³*If parents, who are by nature imperfect and flawed, know how to lovingly take care of their children and give them what they need, how much more will the perfect Heavenly Father give to every one of His children the Holy Spirit's fullness when they ask for Him!"*

Jesus Responds to Controversy

¹⁴One day there was a crowd gathered around Jesus and among them was a man who was mute. Jesus drove the spirit out of the man that made him unable to speak! Once the demon left him, the mute man's tongue was loosed and suddenly, he was able to speak again! The stunned crowd saw it all and marveled in amazement over this miracle! ¹⁵But there were some in the crowd that protested saying, "No wonder He casts out demons! He's doing it in the power of Satan,* the demon-king!" ¹⁶Others were skeptical and tried to persuade Jesus to perform a spectacular display of power to prove that He was the Messiah.†

¹⁷But Jesus, well aware of their every thought, said to them, *"Every divided kingdom that is split against itself is doomed to fail and will eventually collapse. *¹⁸*If it is true that Satan casts out his own demons through Me, then how could his kingdom ever remain intact? *¹⁹*If Satan gives Me the power to cast out his demons, who is it that gives your exorcists‡ their power? Let them become your judges! Go and ask them and they will tell you. *²⁰*Yet if I am casting out demons by God's mighty power§ then the kingdom -realm of God is now released upon you—but you still reject it!¶*

²¹*"Satan's belongings are undisturbed as he stands guard over his fortress-kingdom, strong and fully armed with an arsenal of many weapons. *²²*But when One stronger than he comes to attack and overpower him, the stronger One will empty the arsenal in which he trusted. The Conqueror will ransack his kingdom and distribute all the spoils of victory! *²³*This is a war** and whoever is not on My*

---

* The word used here is *Beelzelbul,* which was an Aramaic word for "the prince of devils" and was worshipped by the Philistines.
† Implied in the context.
‡ Literally, "your sons" which is a figure of speech for their followers.
§ The text literally states, "in the finger of God"—a Hebrew phrase denoting God's power. See Exodus 8:19.
¶ Implied in the context.
** Implied in the context.

side is against Me, and whoever does not gather the spoils with Me will be forever scattered!

²⁴"When a demon is cast out of a person, it wanders in the waterless realm, searching for rest. But finding no place to rest, it says, 'I will go back to the body of the one I left!' ²⁵When it returns, it finds the person like a house that has been swept clean and made tidy, but still empty!* ²⁶Then it goes and enlists seven demons more evil than itself, and they all enter and possess the person, leaving that one with a much worse fate than before!"†

²⁷While He was saying all this, a woman shouted out from the crowd, "God bless the one who gave You birth and nursed You as a child!"

²⁸"Yes," said Jesus, "But God will bless all who listen to the Expression of God‡ and carefully obey everything they hear!"

The Miracle Sign of Jonah the Prophet

²⁹As the crowds began to swell even more, Jesus went on to say, "How evil is this generation! For when you demand a mighty display of power simply to prove who I am, you demonstrate your unbelief!§ The only sign given you will be a repeat of the miracle of Jonah! ³⁰For in the same way Jonah became a sign to the people of Nineveh, so the Son of Man will be a sign to this generation!

³¹"The Queen of Sheba¶ will rise up on the day of judgment to accuse and condemn this generation for its unbelief! She journeyed from a far and distant land just to come and listen to the wisdom of King Solomon. Yet there is One greater than Solomon speaking with you today, but you refuse to listen!** ³²Yes, the people of Nineveh will also rise up on the day of judgment to accuse and condemn this generation! For they all repented when they heard the preaching of Jonah, but you refuse to repent! And there is One greater than Jonah that is preaching to you today!

---

* Implied in the text is the truth that if a person is delivered from a demon, but does not receive Christ and the infilling of the Holy Spirit, their situation can become even worse. True conversion fills a life with Christ and His Spirit.
† Christ's power is still available for all. Even Mary Magdalene had seven demons cast out of her! See Luke 8:2.
‡ Taken from the literal Aramaic text. The Greek word is *logos*.
§ Implied in the context.
¶ Literally, "the Queen of the South." See 1 Kings 10:1-13. Sheba is modern day Yemen.
** Implied in the text here and in v.32.

Revelation-Light

[33]"No one would think of lighting a lamp and then hiding it in their basement where no one would benefit from it. A lamp belongs on a lampstand where all who enter may see its light! [34]The eyes of your spirit allow revelation-light* to enter into your being. When your heart is open, the light floods in!† When your heart is hard and closed, the light cannot penetrate and darkness takes its place. [35]Open your heart and consider My words. Watch out that you do not mistake your opinions for revelation-light! [36]If your spirit burns with light, fully illuminated with no trace of darkness, then you will be a shining lamp—reflecting rays of truth by the way you live!"

Jesus Warns Hypocrites

[37-38]After He had finished saying this, a Jewish religious leader, a Pharisee, asked Him to come for a meal at his home. When they had all been seated at the table, the religious leader was shocked when he noticed that Jesus hadn't performed the cleansing ritual‡ before He began eating. [39]The Lord spoke up and said to him, "You Pharisees are religiously strict in your customs and obsessed with the peripheral issues, like one who will wipe clean only the outside of a cup or bowl, leaving the inside filthy. [40]You are foolish to ignore the greed and wickedness within you! Shouldn't the one who cleans the outside also be concerned with cleaning the inside?§ [41]If you free your heart of greed, showing compassion and true generosity to the poor, then you have more than clean hands; you will be clean within.

[42]"You Pharisees are hopeless frauds! For you are obsessed with peripheral issues, like paying meticulous tithes on the smallest, most insignificant part of your income.¶ These matters you should do, yet when you unjustly cheat others you ignore the most important duty of all— to walk in the love of God! Readjust your values and place first things first!**

---

* The teachings of Jesus are the "revelation-light" referred to here.
† The literal Greek text reads, "Your eye is the lamp of your body. If your eye is healthy, your whole body is full of light; but if it is sick, your body is full of darkness." The "eye" becomes a metaphor for spiritual perception. The "body" is our spirit. The "lamp" is Jesus' teachings. The "darkness" is formed by the lies and opinions that blind us. The translator has chosen to make explicit the metaphors of this passage.
‡ This was not required by the law of Moses, but was a rule imposed by the Pharisees.
§ Translated from the Aramaic text.
¶ Literally, "you pay tithes even on mint and rue and every kind of garden herb"
** Implied in the context.

⁴³*"You Pharisees are hopeless frauds! For you love to be honored before men with your titles of respect, seeking public recognition,* as you aspire to become important among others!*†

⁴⁴*"You Pharisees! What hopeless frauds! Your true character is hidden, like an unmarked grave that hides the corruption inside, defiling all who come in contact with you!"*‡

⁴⁵Just then a specialist in interpreting religious law blurted out, "But Teacher, don't You realize Your words insult me and those of my profession! You're being rude to us all!"

⁴⁶Jesus responded, *"Yes, and you are also hopeless frauds, you experts of the law! For you crush people beneath the burden of obeying impossible religious regulations, yet you would never even think of doing them yourselves!*§ *What hypocrites!* ⁴⁷*What hopeless frauds! You build monuments to honor the prophets of old, yet it was your murdering ancestors that killed them! The only prophet you'll honor is a dead one!*¶ ⁴⁸*In fact, by erecting monuments to the prophets they killed, you demonstrate your agreement with your murdering ancestors and bear witness to their deeds! You're no better than they!* ⁴⁹*That accounts for the wisdom of God saying, 'I will send to them apostles and prophets; though some they will murder and others they will chase away!'* ⁵⁰*This very generation will be held accountable for every drop of blood shed of every murdered prophet from the beginning of time until now!* ⁵¹*That means from the blood of Abel who was killed by his brother, to the blood of Zechariah*** *who was murdered in the middle of the temple court! Yes, the blood-guilt of all your ancestors will be laid before you in this generation!*

⁵²*"So you are nothing but hopeless frauds, you experts of religion! You take away from others the key that opens the door to the house of knowledge. Not only do you lock the door and refuse to enter, you do your best to keep others from the truth!"*

---

* Literally, "greeted with respect in the marketplaces."
† The Aramaic text states, "you aspire to leadership of the synagogues!"
‡ The strictly religious Jew could not touch a dead body or walk over a grave. It was common to whitewash the grave so no one would walk on it and be ceremonially defiled. Jesus is teaching that the people who follow the example of the Pharisees would become morally unclean.
§ The Greek text is literally, "You compel men to carry burdens which you yourselves do not touch."
¶ Implied by the tone and irony of the context.
** II Chronicles 24:21-22. II Chronicles is the last book in the Hebrew order of the Old Testament.

⁵³⁻⁵⁴The religious leaders and experts of the law became enraged and began to furiously oppose Him! They harassed Jesus all the way out the door, spewing out their hostility, arguing over everything He said— trying to entrap Jesus with His own words.

Luke 12

Jesus Warns Against Hypocrisy

[1]By now a crowd of many thousands had gathered around Jesus. So many people pushed to be near Jesus that they began to trample on one another. Jesus turned to His disciples and warned them, *"Make sure you are not influenced by the hypocrisy and phoniness of the religious leaders. It permeates everything they do and teach, for they are merely serving their own interests.** [2]Everything hidden and covered up will soon be exposed! For the façade is falling down and nothing will be kept secret for long!* [3]*Whatever you have spoken in private will be public knowledge, and what you have whispered secretly behind closed doors will be broadcast for all to hear!*

[4]*"Listen, My beloved friends, don't fear those who may want to take your life but nothing more. It's true that they may kill your body, but they have no power over your soul!* [5]*The One you must fear is God, for He has both the power to take your life and the authority to cast your soul into hell.† Yes, the only One you need to fear is God alone!*

[6-7]*"What is the value of your soul to God? Could your worth be defined by an amount of money? God doesn't abandon or forget even the small sparrow He has made. How then could He forget or abandon you? What about the seemingly minor issues of your life? Do they matter to God? Of course they do! You never need to worry, for you are more valuable to God than anything else in this world!‡*

[8]*"I can assure you of this— if you don't hold back, but freely declare in public that I am the Son of Man, the Messiah, then I will freely declare to all the angels of God that you are Mine!* [9]*But if you publicly pretend that you don't know Me, then I will deny you before the angels of God!* [10]*If anyone speaks evil of Me, the Son of Man, they can be forgiven, but if anyone scornfully speaks against the Holy Spirit, it will never be forgiven!* [11]*And*

---

* "Serving their own interests" is found in the Aramaic text.
† The Greek text is literally, "the Valley of Hinnom." This was a valley along the south side of Jerusalem where excrement and rubbish was burned continually. It became a Jewish metaphor for the place of eternal punishment.
‡ The translator has chosen to make explicit the figures of speech and metaphors of these verses. The literal Greek text reads, "Do not five sparrows sell for two copper coins, and not one is overlooked before God. Indeed, the very hairs of your head are numbered. Stop fearing; you are more valuable than many sparrows."

remember this, when they accuse you before everyone* and forcefully drag you before the religious leaders and authorities, do not be troubled. Don't worry about defending yourself or be concerned about how to answer their accusations. ¹²Simply be confident and allow the Holy Spirit access to your heart, and He will reveal in that very moment what you are to say to them."

Jesus Condemns Greed

¹³Just then someone spoke up from the crowd and said, "Master, You should tell my older brother that he has to divide the family inheritance and give me my fair share!"

¹⁴Jesus answered,† "My friend, you can't expect Me to help you with this. It's not My business to settle arguments between you and your brother. That's yours to settle."

¹⁵Then speaking to the people Jesus continued, "Be alert and guard your heart from greed and always wishing for what you don't have! For your life can never be measured by the amount of things you possess!"

¹⁶Jesus gave them this illustration: "A wealthy land owner had a farm that produced bumper crops. In fact, it filled his barns to overflowing! ¹⁷He thought to himself, 'What should I do now that every barn is full and I have nowhere else to store more? ¹⁸I know what I'll do! I'll tear down the barns and build one massive barn that will hold all my grain and goods! ¹⁹Then I can just sit back surrounded with comfort and ease. I'll enjoy life with no worries at all!'

²⁰"But God suddenly spoke to him saying, 'What a fool you are to trust in your riches and not in Me. This very night the messengers of death‡ are demanding to take your life! Then who will get all the wealth you have stored up for yourself?' ²¹This is what will happen to all those who fill up their lives with everything but God!"

Don't Worry

²²Jesus taught His disciples, saying, "Listen to Me. Never let anxiety enter your hearts! Never worry about any of your needs, such as food or clothing. ²³For your life is infinitely more than just food, or the clothing you wear. ²⁴Take the carefree birds as your example; do you ever see them worry? They don't grow their own food or put it in a storehouse for later. Yet God takes care of every one of them, feeding each one of

---

* The Greek text adds, "in the synagogues."
† In the Jewish culture of that day, rabbis would be asked to mediate disputes such as this, but this man did not want mediation, but representation.
‡ The Greek text is simply "they."

them from His love and goodness. Isn't your life more precious to God than a bird's? Be carefree in the care of God!*

²⁵"*Does worry add anything to your life? Can it add one more year, or even one day?* ²⁶ *So if worrying adds nothing, but actually subtracts from your life, then why would you worry about God's care of you?*

²⁷"*Think about the lilies. They grow and become beautiful, not because they work hard or strive to clothe themselves. Yet not even Solomon, wearing his kingly garments of splendor, could be compared to a field of lilies.* ²⁸*So if God can clothe the fields and meadows with grass and flowers, can't He clothe you as well, O struggling one with so many doubts?*† ²⁹*I repeat it: Don't let worry enter your life! Live above the anxious cares about your personal needs!* ³⁰*People everywhere seem to worry about making a living, but Your heavenly Father knows your every need and will take care of you.* ³¹*Each and every day He will supply your needs as you seek His kingdom passionately above all else!* ³²*So don't ever be afraid, dearest friends. Your loving Father joyously gives you His kingdom-realm with all its promises!*

³³"*Go and sell what you have and give to those in need, making deposits in your account in heaven, an account that will never be taken from you. Your gifts will become a secure and unfailing treasure, deposited in heaven forever.* ³⁴*Where you deposit your treasure is where your thoughts will turn to— and your heart will long to be there also!*

Be Ready

³⁵"*Be prepared and ready for action*‡ *at a moment's notice.* ³⁶*Be like the servants who anticipate their master's return from the wedding celebration. They'll be ready to unlock and open the door for him at a moment's notice!* ³⁷*What great joy is ahead for the awakened ones who are waiting for the Master's return! He Himself will become their Servant and wait on them at His table as He passes by!* ³⁸*He may appear at midnight or even later, but what great joy for the awakened ones whenever He comes!* ³⁹*Of course, if they knew ahead of time the hour of the Master's appearing they would be alert, just as they would be ready if they knew ahead of time that a thief was coming to break into their house!* ⁴⁰*So keep being awakened and ready at all times. For I can promise you that the Son of Man will surprise you and will appear*§ *just when you don't expect Him!*"

---

* Implied in the context.

† This is one Greek word that means, "little-faiths."

‡ The Greek is literally, "Let your loins be girded and keep your lamps burning."

§ The Greek word can more accurately be translated, "become."

The Faithful Servant

⁴¹"Lord," Peter asked, "Does this apply only to the Twelve of us, or is it for everyone else as well?"

⁴²And the Lord said, "*A trustworthy and thoughtful manager who understands the ways of his Master, will be given a ministry of responsibility in his Master's house, serving others exactly what they need at just the right time.* ⁴³⁻⁴⁴*And when the Master returns He will find that His servant has served Him well. I can promise you, he will be given a great reward and will be placed as an overseer of everything the Master owns!*

⁴⁵"*But if that servant says in his heart, 'My Master delays His coming; who knows when He will be returning!' Then because of this delay, he elevates himself and begins to mistreat those in his Master's household. Instead of caring for the ones he was appointed to serve, he begins to abuse the other servants—both men and women. He also begins to throw drunken parties for his friends and give himself over to every pleasure.* ⁴⁶*Let me tell you what will happen to him! His Master will suddenly return at a time that shocks him and He will remove the abusive, selfish servant from his position of trust. He will be severely punished and assigned a portion with the unbelievers!*

⁴⁷"*And every servant who knows full well what pleases his Master, and who does not make himself ready and refuses to put his Master's will to action, he will be punished with many blows!* ⁴⁸*But the servant who does not know his Master's will* * *and unwittingly does what is wrong; he will be punished less severely. For those who have received a greater revelation from their Master will be required a greater obedience. And those who have been entrusted with great responsibility will be held more responsible to their Master.*

Jesus Brings Fire to the Earth

⁴⁹"*I have come to set the earth on fire! And how I long for every heart to be already ablaze with this fiery passion for God!* ⁵⁰*But first I must be immersed into the baptism of God's judgment,*† *and I am consumed with passion as I await its fulfillment!* ⁵¹*Don't think for a moment that I came to grant peace and harmony to everyone. No, for My coming will change everything and create hostility among you.* ⁵²*From now on, even family members will be divided over Me, and will choose sides*‡ *against one another!* ⁵³*Fathers will be split off against sons and sons against fathers, mothers will be against*

---

* Implied in the text.

† The implication of the context is that Jesus is drawing closer to His time of experiencing God's judgment for our sins on the cross. It is a "baptism" of judgment which we deserved.

‡ The Greek text is literally, "among five in one house, three will be against two and two will be against three."

daughters and daughters against mothers, mother-in-laws will be against brides and brides against mother-in-laws—all because of Me!"

Discerning the Time

[54]Then Jesus said to the crowds gathered around Him, *"When you see a cloud forming in the west don't you say, 'A storm is brewing?' And then it arrives.* [55]*And when you feel the south wind blowing you say, 'A heat wave is on the way.' And so it happens.* [56]*But what hypocrites!* * *You are such experts at forecasting the weather, but are totally unwilling to understand the spiritual significance[†] of the very time you're living in!*

[57]*"You can't even judge for yourselves what is good and right!* [58]*For when you are wrong, it is better that you agree with your adversary and settle your dispute before you have to go before a judge. If not, you may be dragged into court, and the judge may find you guilty and* [59]*throw you into prison until you have paid off your fine entirely!"*

---

* There is an amazing play on words found in the Aramaic text. The word for "hypocrites" is literally, "acceptor of faces." The Aramaic states they looked at the "face" of the sky and "faces" of men, living superficially, not seeing what was happening spiritually around them.
† Implied in the context.

Luke 13

The Need for True Repentance

¹Some of those present informed Jesus that Pilate had slaughtered some Galilean Jews* while they were offering sacrifices at the temple, mixing their blood with the sacrifices they were offering. ²Then He turned and asked the crowd, *"Do you believe that the slaughtered Galileans were the worst sinners of all the other Galileans? ³No they weren't! So listen to Me— unless you all repent,† you will perish as they did! ⁴Or what about the eighteen who perished when the tower of Siloam‡ fell upon them? Do you really think that they were guiltier than all of the others in Jerusalem? ⁵No they weren't. But unless you repent you will all eternally perish just as they did!"*

The Parable of the Barren Tree

⁶Then Jesus told them this parable: *"There was a man who planted a fig tree in his orchard but when he came to gather fruit from his tree, he found none for it was barren and had no fruit. ⁷So he said to his gardener, 'For the last three years I've come to gather figs from my tree, but it remains fruitless. What a waste! Go ahead and cut it down!' ⁸But the gardener insisted and said, 'Sir, we should leave it one more year. Let me fertilize and cultivate it, and then let's see if it will produce fruit. ⁹If it doesn't bear fruit by next year, we'll cut it down!'"§*

---

* It is likely that Pilate viewed these Jews as rebellious to his rule. This was indeed an atrocious act by Pilate.

† The Greek term for repentance means, "to change your mind and amend your ways."

‡ Siloam was the name of a pool or reservoir for the city of Jerusalem near the junction of the south and east walls of the city.

§ This parable was an obvious picture of the nation of Israel. The owner was the Father and the gardener was Jesus who had come to them and for three years had longed to have true spiritual fruit from His spiritual vine (Isaiah 5:1-7). The warning is that it would be cut down if it did not bear the fruit of repentance. The purpose of the parable was to warn them that they were in their last year of God's grace toward them.

Jesus Heals on the Sabbath Day

[10]One Sabbath day while Jesus was teaching in the Jewish meeting house, [11]He encountered a seriously handicapped woman. She was crippled and had been doubled over for eighteen years. It was caused by a demonic spirit of bondage* that had left her totally unable to stand up straight. [12-13]When Jesus saw her condition, He called her over and gently laid His hands upon her. Then He said to her, *"Dear woman, you are free! I release you forever from this crippling spirit!"* Instantly she could stand straight and tall and began to overflow with glorious praise to God!

[14]But the local Jewish leader who was in charge of the meeting house was infuriated over Jesus healing on the Sabbath day! "Six days you are to work", he shouted out angrily to the crowd, "Those are the days you should come here for healing, but not on the seventh day!"

[15]Then the Lord spoke up and said, *"You hopeless frauds, overly critical and splitting hairs! Don't you care for your animals on the Sabbath day, untying your ox or donkey from the stall and leading it away to water?* [16]*If you do this for your animals, then what's wrong with allowing this beloved daughter of Abraham, who has been bound by Satan for eighteen long years, to be untied and set free on a Sabbath day?"*

[17]When they heard this, His critics were completely humiliated as the crowds shouted with joy over the glorious things Jesus was doing among them!

Parables of Jesus

[18]Then Jesus taught them this parable: *"How can I truly describe the kingdom-realm of God? Let me illustrate it this way.* [19]*It is like the smallest of seeds that you would plant in a garden. And yet when it grows, it becomes a huge tree with so many spreading branches that various birds† make nests there."*

[20]And again Jesus taught them another parable: *"How could I truly describe the kingdom-realm of God? Let me give you this illustration:* [21]*It is like something as small as yeast that a woman kneads into a large amount of dough. It works unseen until it permeates‡ the entire batch and rises high."*

---

* Literally, "spirit of weakness."

† See Ezekiel 17:23. The obvious meaning of this parable is that the kingdom of God will begin small but it will expand, grow, and mature. People from every nation will come and make a "nest" in the kingdom of God.

‡ The central meaning of this parable focuses on how something small impacts and penetrates something great. It is the pervading influence of virtue and truth that is highlighted here. There is a transformation taking place as the hidden, yet pervasive, kingdom begins to impact every part of culture and society around us.

The Ways of the Kingdom-Realm

²²Jesus ministered in one town and village after another,* teaching the people as He made His way toward Jerusalem. ²³A bystander asked Him, "Lord, will only a few have eternal life?" Jesus then said to the crowd, ²⁴*"There is a great cost† for anyone to enter through the narrow doorway to the kingdom-realm of God. For I can tell you, there will be many who will want to enter but won't be able. ²⁵For once the Head of the house has shut and locked the door, it will be too late! Even if you stand outside knocking, begging to enter and saying, 'Lord, Lord, open the door for us!' Yet He will say to you, 'I don't know who you are! You are not a part of My family!'*‡

²⁶*"Then you will reply, 'But Lord, we dined with You, and walked with You as You taught us.' ²⁷And He will reply, 'Don't you understand? I don't have a clue who you are, for you are not a part of My family. You cannot enter in. Now go away from Me! For you are all disloyal to Me and do evil!'*§

²⁸*"Then you will experience great weeping and great anguish as you see Abraham, Isaac, and Jacob along with all the prophets of Israel enjoying the kingdom of God while you yourselves are barred from entering! ²⁹And you will see people streaming from the four corners of the earth, accepting the invitation to feast in God's kingdom -realm while you are kept outside¶ looking in. ³⁰Take note of this: There are some who are despised and viewed as the least important now, but one day they will be placed at the head of the line. And there are others who are viewed as 'elite' today that will become least important then."*

Jesus' Sorrow for Jerusalem

³¹Just then some Jewish religious leaders came to Jesus to inform Him that Herod was out to kill Him and that He should flee from that place. ³²Jesus told them, *"Go and tell that 'deceiver'** that I will continue to cast out demons and heal the sick until I am ready to complete My ministry and fulfill My*

---

* Jesus now visits the places where His disciples had already been sent to. See Luke 10:1-11.
† The Greek word used here is actually, "agonize."
‡ Implied in the text.
§ This is quoted from Psalm 6:8. Though they were acquaintances, they had not responded to His message with repentance. The word *disloyal* is taken from the Aramaic. The question to ask is not simply, "Will the saved be few?" (v.23) but rather, "Will it be you?"
¶ Implied in the text.
** The word literally means, "fox."

purpose. ³³*For yet a brief season everyone knows I am safe until I come to Jerusalem, for that is where all the prophets have been killed.* ³⁴*O city of Jerusalem, you are the city that murders your prophets! You are the city that pelts to death with stones the very messengers* who were sent to deliver you! So many times I have longed to gather your wayward children together around Me, as a hen gathers her chicks under her wings— but you were too stubborn to let Me!* ³⁵*And now, it is too late since your house will be left in ruins.† You will not see Me again until you are able to say, 'We welcome the One who comes to us in the name of the Lord!'" ‡*

---

* Or, "apostles."
† See Jeremiah 12:7.
‡ See Psalm 118:26.

Luke 14

Jesus Heals Again on the Sabbath

[1]One day Jesus was on His way to dine with a prominent Jewish religious leader for a Sabbath meal. Everyone was watching Him to see if He would heal anyone on the Sabbath. [2]Just then standing right in front of Him was a man suffering with his limbs swollen with fluid. [3]Jesus asked the experts of the Law and the Pharisees who were present, *"Is it permitted within the Law to heal a man on the Sabbath day? Is it right or wrong?"* [4]Yet no one dared to answer. Jesus turned to the sick man, took hold of him, and instantly released healing to him, and sent him on his way. [5]Jesus said to them all, *"If one of your children or one of your animals fell into a well, wouldn't you do all you could to rescue them even if it was a Sabbath day?"* [6]There was nothing they could say—all were silenced!

Humility and Hospitality

[7]When Jesus noticed how the guests for the meal were all vying for the seats of honor, He shared this story with the guests around the table: [8]*"When you are invited to an important social function, don't be quick to sit near the head of the table, choosing the seat of honor. What will happen when someone more distinguished than you arrives? [9]The host will bring him over to where you are sitting and ask for your seat, saying in front of all the guests, 'You're in the wrong place; please give this person your seat.' Disgraced, you will have to take whatever seat is left. [10]But instead, when you're invited to the banquet, you should choose to sit down in the lowest place* so that when your host comes and sees you there, he may say, 'My friend, come with me and let me seat you in a better place.' And then in front of all the other guests at the banquet, you will be honored and seated in the place of highest respect. [11]Remember this: Everyone with a lofty opinion of who they are and those who seek to raise themselves up will be humbled before all. And everyone with a modest opinion of who they are and those who choose to humble themselves will be raised up before all."*

---

* See Proverbs 25:6-7.

¹²Then Jesus turned to His host and said, *"When you throw a banquet, don't just invite your friends, relatives, or rich neighbors—for it is likely they will return the favor.* ¹³⁻¹⁴*It is better to invite those who never get an invitation. Invite the poor to your banquet, along with the outcast, the handicapped and the blind— those who could never repay you the favor. Then you will experience a great blessing in this life and at the resurrection of the godly, you will receive a full reward!"*

¹⁵When they heard this one of the dinner guests said to Jesus, "Someday God will have a kingdom feast* and how happy and privileged will be the ones who get to share in that joy!"

¹⁶Jesus replied with this parable, *"There was a Man who invited many to join Him in a great feast.* ¹⁷*As the day arrived for the feast, the Host instructed His servant to notify all the invited guests and tell them, 'Come, for everything is now ready for you!'* ¹⁸*But one by one, they all began to make excuses. One said, 'I can't come. I just bought some property and I'm obligated to go and look it over.'* ¹⁹*Another said, 'Please accept my regrets for I just purchased five teams of oxen† and I need to make sure they can pull the plow.'* ²⁰*And yet another one said, 'I can't come because I just got married.'* ²¹*And the servant reported back to the Host and told Him of all their excuses. The Master became angry and said to His servant, 'Then go at once throughout the city and invite anyone you find—the poor, the blind, the disabled, the hurting, and the lonely— and invite them to My banquet.* ²²*The servant then returned to his Master saying, 'Sir, I have done what you've asked, but there's still room for more.'* ²³*So the Master told him, 'Alright. Now go out again and this time bring them all back with you! Persuade the beggars on the streets, the outcasts, even the homeless— go and urgently insist that they come in and enjoy the feast so that My house will be full!*

²⁴*"So I say to you all, the one who receives an invitation to feast with Me and makes excuses, will never enjoy My banquet!"*

The Cost of Following Jesus

²⁵As massive crowds followed Jesus, He turned to them and said these words: ²⁶*"When you follow Me as My disciple you will appear to others as though you were one who hates your father, your mother, your wife, your sisters, your brothers—yes, even seeming as one who hates your own life! This is the price you'll pay to be considered as one of My followers!* ²⁷*And anyone who comes to Me must be willing to share My cross and experience it as their own, or they cannot be considered*

---

* The guest at the dinner assumed the kingdom of God was coming one day, but Jesus' parable explains that it has begun already with the invitation to come to Him, the King!

† This implies he was a wealthy man who foolishly chose possessions over Christ.

to be My disciple! ²⁸So don't follow Me without considering what it will cost you! For who would construct a house* before first sitting down to estimate the cost to complete it? ²⁹Otherwise he may lay the foundation and not be able to finish. The neighbors will ridicule him saying, ³⁰'Look at the silly fool! He started to build, but couldn't complete it!'

³¹"Have you ever heard of a commander† who goes out to war without first sitting down with strategic planning to determine the strength of his army to win the war‡ against a stronger opponent? ³²If he knows he doesn't stand a chance of winning the war, the wise commander will send out delegates to negotiate the terms of peace. ³³Likewise, unless you surrender all to Me, giving up all you possess, you cannot be one of My disciples.

³⁴"Salt is good for seasoning. But if salt were to lose its flavor, there would be no way to regain it. ³⁵Its only benefit§ is to be discarded!¶ If you have ears opened by the Spirit, then hear the meaning of what I have said and apply it to yourselves!"**

---

* Or, "tower."
† Or, "king."
‡ The Greek text states, "with 10,000 he will be able to go up against 20,000."
§ The Greek text states, "It will not be fit for the soil or for the manure pile."
¶ Followers of Jesus who are unwilling to pay the price of discipleship are like worthless salt, unable to affect anything or anyone!
** Implied in the text.

Luke 15

The Parable of the Lost Lamb

¹Many dishonest tax collectors and other notorious sinners often gathered around to listen as Jesus taught the people. ²This raised concerns with the Jewish religious leaders and experts of the law. Indignant, they began to grumble and complain saying, "Look at how this Man associates with all these notorious sinners and welcomes them to come to Him!"

³In response Jesus gave them this illustration: ⁴⁻⁵*"There once was a Shepherd with one hundred lambs, but one of His lambs wandered away and was lost. So the Shepherd left the ninety-nine lambs out in the open field as He searched and searched in the wilderness for that one lost lamb, and He didn't stop until He finally found it! With exuberant joy He raised it up and placed it on His shoulders,* carrying it back with cheerful delight! ⁶Returning home, He called all His friends and neighbors together and said, 'Let's have a party! Come and celebrate with Me the return of My lost lamb! It wandered away, but I found it and brought it home!'"*

⁷Jesus continued, *"In the same way, there will be a glorious celebration in heaven over the rescue of one lost sinner who repents, comes back home, and returns to the fold— more so than for all the righteous people who never strayed away."*

The Parable of the Lost Coin

⁸Then Jesus gave them another parable: *"There once was a woman who had ten † valuable silver coins. When she lost one of them, she swept her entire house, diligently searching every corner of her house for that one lost silver coin. ⁹And when she finally found it, she gathered all her friends and neighbors for a celebration, telling them, 'Come and celebrate with me! I had lost my precious silver coin, but now I've found*

---

* What a wonderful picture this gives us of our Shepherd. He doesn't beat the lost sheep for wandering away. He raises it up and carries it home!

† The silver coin was a *zuza* (Aramaic). Although there are differing opinions as to its value, it could be equal in today's currency to about $1.200. Notice the change of numbers in the three parables found in this chapter: one out of a hundred for the sheep, one out of ten for the coins, and one out of two for the sons. This shows—progressively—the extraordinary value that Jesus places on every lost soul.

it!"* ¹⁰That's the same way God responds every time one lost sinner repents and turns to Him. He says to all His angels, 'Let's have a joyous celebration, for that one which was lost, I have found!'"

The Parable of the Loving Father

¹¹Then Jesus said, *"Once there was a Father with two sons.* ¹²*The younger son came to his Father and said, "Father, don't you think that it's time to give me the share of your estate that belongs to me?†* So the Father went ahead and distributed among His two sons their inheritance. ¹³*Shortly afterwards, the younger son packed up all his belongings and travelled off to see the world. He journeyed to a far off land where he soon wasted all he was given in a binge of extravagant and reckless living!*

¹⁴*"Now with everything spent and nothing left, he soon grew hungry, for there was a severe famine in that land.* ¹⁵*He begged a farmer in that country to hire him, and the farmer hired him and sent him out to feed the pigs!* ¹⁶*The hungry son was so famished, that he was willing to even eat the slop given to the pigs,‡ because no one would feed him a thing!*

¹⁷*"Humiliated, the son finally realized what he was doing and he thought to himself, 'There are so many workers at my Father's house who have all the food they want with plenty to spare! They lack nothing! Why am I here dying of hunger, feeding these pigs, and eating their slop?* ¹⁸*I will go back home to my Father's house and I'll say to Him, "Father, I was so wrong! I have sinned against You!* ¹⁹*I'll never be worthy to be called Your son again. Please Father, just treat me like one of Your employees."'*

²⁰*"So the young son set off for home, to his Father's house. But from a long distance away, His Father saw him coming dressed as a beggar§ and great compassion swelled up in His heart for His Son who was returning home. So the Father ran out to meet him! He swept him up in His arms, hugged him closely, and kissed him over and over with tender love!*

---

* The valuable silver coin had an image of Roman authority stamped upon it. We have been stamped with the image of God. Even when we are "lost," that image is still present, needing only to be "found" by grace and redeemed.

† In Middle Eastern cultures, it was a great offense for the son to ask his father for his inheritance. It would be equal to saying, "I wish you were already dead!"

‡ This would be degrading to anyone, but especially a Jew who was forbidden to raise swine.

§ Implied in the context of the Greek text and stated more explicitly in the Aramaic.

²¹"Then the son spoke up and said, 'Father, I was so wrong! I have sinned against You! I could never deserve to be called Your son, just let me be...' But the Father interrupted,* saying, 'Son, you're home now!'

²²"Turning to His servants, the Father said, 'Quick, bring Me the robe, the splendid robe of favor, and place it upon his shoulders! Bring the ring, the seal of sonship,† and put it upon his finger! And bring out the best clothes‡ you can find for My son! ²³Prepare a great feast§ and let's all celebrate! ²⁴For this beloved son of mine was once dead, but now he's alive again! Once he was lost, but now He is found!' And every one began to celebrate with overflowing joy!

²⁵"Now the older son was out working in the field when his brother returned and as he approached the house he could hear the music of celebration and dancing! ²⁶So he called over one of the servants and asked, 'What's going on?' ²⁷The servant replied, 'It's your younger brother! He's returned home and your Father is throwing a party to celebrate his homecoming!' ²⁸Then the older son became angry and refused to go in and celebrate, so his Father came out to plead with him, 'Come and enjoy the feast with us!'¶ ²⁹But the son said, 'Father, listen! How many years have I been working like a slave for you, performing every duty You've asked, as a faithful son?** I've never once disobeyed You, but You've never thrown a party for me because of my faithfulness. Never once have you even given me a goat that I could feast and celebrate with my friends like he's doing now! ³⁰But look at this 'son' of yours! He comes back after wasting your wealth on prostitutes and reckless living, and here You are throwing a great feast to celebrate—for him!'

³¹"Then the Father said to him, 'My son, you are always with Me by My side. Everything I have is yours to enjoy. ³²It's only right to celebrate like this and be overjoyed, because this brother of yours was once dead and gone, but now he is alive and back with us again! He was lost, but now he is found!'"

---

* This poetic description is added to enhance the cultural and spiritual meaning of the text.

† Culturally, this ring was an emblem of authority giving the son authority to transact business in the father's name.

‡ Implied in the context. The Greek text is, "bring sandals for his feet." Slaves were barefoot.

§ Implied in the text. The Greek text is, "kill the grain-fatted calf."

¶ In the culture of that era, hospitality was of supreme importance. To refuse to go in to the feast, when culturally, it was his responsibility to co-host the event with his father, was a humiliating rejection to the father.

** While the younger brother pursued self-discovery, the older brother was one who believed in moral conformity, earning favor from his father. Both needed the revelation of grace.

Luke 16

The Story of the Dishonest Manager

¹Jesus taught His disciples using this story: "*There was once a very rich man who hired a manager to run his business and oversee all his wealth. But soon a rumor began to spread that the manager was wasting his master's money.* ²*So the master called him in and said, "Is it true that you are mismanaging my estate? You need to provide me with a complete audit of everything you oversee for me. I've decided to dismiss you.*

³*"Then the manager thought to himself, 'Now what am I going to do? I'm finished here! I can't hide what I've done,* ⃰ *and I'm too proud to beg to get my job back.'* ⁴*I have an idea that will secure my future. It will win me favor and secure friends who can take care of me and help me when I get fired!'* ⁵*So the dishonest manager hatched his scheme. He went to everyone who owed his master money, one by one, and he asked them, 'How much do you owe my master?'* ⁶⁻⁷*One debtor owed $20,000 so he said to him, 'Let me see your bill. Pay me now and we'll settle for twenty percent less.' In this way, the clever manager scratched out the original amount owed and reduced it by twenty percent.' To another who owed $200,000, he said, 'Pay me now and we'll reduce your bill by fifty percent.' And the clever manager scratched out the original amount owed and reduced it by half.*

⁸*Even though his master was defrauded, when he found out about the shrewd way this manager had feathered his own nest, he congratulated the clever scoundrel for what he'd done to lay up for his future needs.*"

Jesus continued, "*Remember this: The sons of darkness are shrewder than the sons of light are in their interactions with others.* ⁹*It is important that you use the wealth of this world to demonstrate your friendship with God by winning friends and blessing others. Then, when this world fails and falls apart, your generosity will provide you with an eternal reward!*"†

---

* The manager's words include an ancient Aramaic figure of speech, "I can't dig" which means, it can't be buried or hidden.
† Or, "You will be welcomed to the tents of eternity."

¹⁰"The one who manages the little they have been given with faithfulness and integrity will be promoted and trusted with greater responsibilities. But those who cheat with the little they have been given will not be considered trustworthy to receive more. ¹¹If you have not handled the riches of this world with integrity, why should you be trusted with the eternal treasures of the spiritual world? ¹²And if you've not been proven faithful with what belongs to another, why should you be given wealth of your own? ¹³It is simply impossible for a person to serve two masters at the same time. You will be forced to love one and reject the other. One master will be despised and the other will have your loyal devotion. It is no different with God and the wealth of this world.* You must enthusiastically love one—and definitively reject the other!"

¹⁴Now the Jewish religious leaders who were listening to Jesus were lovers of money. They laughed at what He said and mocked His teachings. ¹⁵So Jesus addressed them directly, "You always want to look 'spiritual' in the eyes of others, but you have forgotten the eyes of God which see what is inside you! The very things that you approve of and applaud are the very things God despises! ¹⁶The laws of Moses and the revelation of the prophets have prepared you for the arrival of the kingdom-realm announced by John. And now when this wonderful news of the kingdom-realm of God is preached, people's hearts burn with extreme passion to press in and receive it! ¹⁷Heaven and earth will disintegrate before even the smallest detail of the word of God will fail or lose its power!

¹⁸"It is wrong for you to divorce to cover your lust for another wife! That is adultery! And when you take that one you have lusted after as your wife, and contribute to the breakup of her marriage, you are once again guilty of adultery!"

The Rich Man and Lazarus

¹⁹Jesus continued: "There once was a very rich man who had the finest things imaginable,† living every day enjoying his life of opulent luxury! ²⁰⁻²¹Outside the gate of his mansion‡ was a poor beggar named Lazarus.§ He lay there every day covered with boils and the neighborhood dogs would come and lick his open sores. The only food he had to eat was the garbage that the rich man threw away. ²²One day poor Lazarus died and the angels of God came and escorted his spirit into paradise.¶ ²³Later the day came that the rich man also died. In hell he looked up from his torment and saw

---

* The word used here is "mammon" which is money personified as a god that is worshipped.
† The Greek text is literally, "he was dressed in a purple robe." This is a figure of speech that refers to the luxury that surrounded him. This was the kind of robe worn only by kings.
‡ Implied by the context.
§ Lazarus is a form of the name *Eleazar*, and means, "God is my help."
¶ The Greek text is literally, "Abraham's bosom" which is a metaphor for paradise.

Abraham in the distance and Lazarus the beggar standing beside him in the glory! ²⁴'So the rich man shouted out, 'Father Abraham! Father Abraham! Have mercy on me! Send Lazarus to dip his finger in water and come to cool my tongue for I am in agony in these flames of fire!'

²⁵"But Abraham responded: 'My friend, don't you remember how while you were alive, you had all you desired, surrounded in luxury while Lazarus had nothing? Now Lazarus is in the comforts of paradise and you are in agony. ²⁶But besides this, between us is a huge chasm that cannot be bridged, keeping anyone from crossing from one realm to the other, even if they wanted to!'

²⁷"So the rich man said, 'Then let me ask you, Father Abraham; please send Lazarus to my relatives! ²⁸Tell him to witness to my five brothers and warn them not to end up where I am in this place of torment!' ²⁹But Abraham replied, 'They already have enough warning. They have the teachings of Moses and the prophets and they must obey them!'

³⁰'But what if they're not listening?' the rich man added, 'If someone from the dead were to go and warn them, they would surely repent!' ³¹But Abraham said to him, 'If they won't listen to Moses and the prophets neither would they believe even if Someone* were raised from the dead!'"

---

* Translated from the Aramaic. Jesus is that "Someone" who rose from the grave, yet many still will not listen and believe.

Luke 17

Jesus Teaches on Faith and Forgiveness

¹One day Jesus taught His disciples: *"Betrayals* are inevitable, but great devastation will come to the one guilty of betraying others!* ²*It would be better for him to have a heavy boulder tied around his neck and be hurled into the deepest sea than to face the punishment of betraying one of My dear ones! So be alert to your brother's condition* ³*and if you see him going the wrong direction, cry out and correct him. And if there is true repentance on his part, forgive him.* ⁴*And no matter how many times in one day your brother sins against you† and says, 'I am sorry— I am changing; forgive me,' you still need to forgive him each and every time."*

⁵Upon hearing this, the apostles asked Jesus, "Lord, You must please increase‡ our measure of faith!"

⁶Jesus responded, *"If you have even the smallest measure of authentic faith, it would be powerful enough to say to this large§ tree— 'My faith will pull you up by the roots and throw you into the sea!'—and it will respond to your faith and obey you!"¶*

⁷⁻⁸Jesus continued, *"After a servant has finished his work in the field or with the livestock, he doesn't just immediately sit down to relax and eat. No, a true servant prepares the food for his master first and makes sure his master is served his meal before he sits down to eat his own.* ⁹*Does the true servant expect to be thanked for doing what is required of him?* ¹⁰*So learn this lesson: After doing all that is commanded of you, simply say, 'We are mere servants, undeserving of special praise, for we are just doing what is expected of us and fulfilling our duties.'"*

---

* From the Aramaic. Other Greek texts use "temptation" or, "to stumble."
† The Greek text states explicitly, "seven times." But this is used as a metaphor for unlimited forgiveness.
‡ The Greek text is literally, "add faith to us."
§ The Greek text is, "mulberry" or "sycamore tree," known to grow to about thirty-five feet high.
¶ Implied conclusion of the text. The apostles had faith, but simply needed to use it!

Jesus Heals Ten Lepers

¹¹Jesus traveled on toward Jerusalem and passed through the border region between Samaria and Galilee. ¹²As He entered one village ten men approached Him, but they kept their distance, for they were lepers. ¹³They shouted out to Him, "Mighty Lord, our Wonderful Master!* Won't You have mercy on us and heal us?"† ¹⁴When Jesus stopped to look at them, He simply spoke these words, *"Go to be examined by the Jewish priests‡ and you will discover that you are healed!"§* As they set off they were healed while walking along the way!

¹⁵Then one of them, who was a foreigner from Samaria,¶ when he discovered that he was completely healed, turned back to find Jesus, and began shouting out his joyous praises and glorified God! ¹⁶When he found Jesus, he fell down at His feet and thanked Him over and over, and said to Him: "You are the Messiah."**

¹⁷*"So where are the other nine?"* Jesus replied, *"Weren't there ten who were healed?* ¹⁸*They refused to return to give thanks and give glory to God except you, a foreigner from Samaria!"* ¹⁹Then Jesus said to the healed man, laying at His feet, *"Arise and go! It was your faith that brought you salvation and healing!"*

God's Kingdom-Realm Within You

²⁰Jesus was once asked by the Jewish religious leaders, "When will the kingdom-realm of God come?"††

Jesus responded and told them, *"The kingdom-realm of God does not come simply by obeying principles‡‡ or by waiting for signs. ²¹The kingdom-realm is not discovered in one place or another, for the kingdom of God is already within some of you!"§§*

---

* The Greek word used here for "Master" is not the usual word used for "Teacher" or "Master." It denotes one with supernatural authority and power.
† It is implied that they were seeking a healing from Jesus.
‡ This was what was required. See Leviticus 13:19; 14:1–11.
§ They were to go to the priest, who would confirm their healing and declare them ceremonially clean and approved to go into the temple to worship God.
¶ This information is supplied from v. 16. For a Samaritan man to give thanks to a Jewish man was indeed peculiar. Since he likely had no "priest," he turned to the only One he knew to be a priest for him, Jesus Christ.
** From the Aramaic text.
†† Or, "When will God's kingdom be established?"
‡‡ Implied in the Aramaic text where it states, "observances (of the law)." The same word is found in Galatians 4:10 referring to "observances" of keeping the law.
§§ Translated from the Aramaic text.

²²Later, Jesus continued to address this with His apostles, saying: *"The time is coming when a great passion will be awakened within you to see Me again. Yes, you will long to see the beginning of the days of the Son of Man, but you won't be able to find Me.* ²³*And you will hear reports from some who will say, 'Look, He has returned!' 'He's over here,' or, 'He's over there!' But don't believe it or run after them for their claims will be false.** ²⁴*The day of the Son of Man will burst forth with the brightness of a lightning strike that shines from one end of the sky to the other, illuminating the earth!*

²⁵*"But before this takes place the Son of Man must pass through great suffering and rejection from this generation.* ²⁶*The very same things that happened in the days of Noah will take place in the days of the Son of Man:* ²⁷*The people lived their lives thinking that nothing had changed. They got married and raised families, not realizing what was coming until the very day that Noah boarded the ark and the devastating flood came and swept them all away!* ²⁸⁻³⁰*And the days of the Son of Man can be compared to the days of Lot. The people of that time lived their lives as normal. They got married, raised families, built homes and businesses, yet they were totally unaware of what was coming until the very day Lot departed from Sodom. The sky opened up and rained fire and burning sulfur upon them—destroying everyone and everything they had built! And so it will be on the day of the unveiling of the Son of Man!*

³¹*In the day of My appearing, if one is out working in the yard,† he won't even have time to go back into the house to gather his belongings. And those toiling in their fields won't have time to run back home.* ³²*Don't forget the example of Lot's wife and what happened to her when she turned back!‡* ³³*All who are obsessed with being secure in life will lose it all— including their life. But those who let go of their life and surrender it to Me, will discover true life!* ³⁴*For in that night there will be two lying in their bed; one will be swept suddenly away in judgment while the other will be left alive.* ³⁵⁻³⁶*There will be two women working together at household duties and one will be swept suddenly away in judgment while the other will be left§ alive!"¶*

³⁷Then His apostles asked, "But Lord, where will this judgment** happen?"

---

* Implied in the context.

† The Greek text is literally, "on the roof."

‡ Genesis 19:26.

§ This Greek word can also refer to being "forgiven of sin."

¶ Some later Greek texts add, "Two men will be in the field; one will be taken and the other will be left."

** Implied in the context.

And Jesus responded, *"It will be obvious,** *for wherever there are those spiritually dead,*† *there you will find the eagles circling."*

---

* Implied in the context.
† The Greek word here is literally "corpse," and can be a metaphor for those who are spiritually dead.

Luke 18

A Widow Who Wouldn't Stop Asking

¹One day Jesus taught them to keep praying and never stop, or lose hope. He shared with them this illustration: ²*"In a certain town there was a civil judge, a thick-skinned and godless man who had no fear of other's opinions.* ³*And there was a poor widow in that town who kept pleading and pleading with the judge, 'Grant me justice and protect me against my oppressor!'* ⁴⁻⁵*He ignored her pleas for quite some time, but she kept asking. Eventually he said to himself, 'This widow keeps annoying me, demanding for her rights and I'm tired of listening to her. Even though I'm not a religious man and don't care about the opinions of others, I'll just get her off my back and answer her claims for justice, and I'll rule in her favor. Then she'll leave me alone!'*

⁶So the Lord continued, *"Did you hear what the ungodly judge said— that he would answer her persistent request?* ⁷*Don't you know that God, the True Judge, will grant justice to all His chosen ones who cry out to Him night and day? He will pour out His Spirit upon them!* He will not delay to answer you and give you what you ask for!* ⁸*God will give swift justice to those who don't give up. Yet when the Son of Man comes back, will He find this kind of persistent faithfulness in His people?"*

Humility in Prayer

⁹Jesus taught this parable to those who were convinced they were morally upright and trusted in their own virtue, yet looked down on others with disgust: ¹⁰*"Once there were two men who went into the temple to pray. One was a proud religious leader, the other a despised tax collector.* ¹¹⁻¹²*The religious leader stood apart from the others and prayed, 'How I thank You, O God, that I'm not wicked like everyone else! They're cheaters, swindlers, and crooks— like that tax collector over there. God, You know that I never cheat, or commit adultery; I fast from food twice a week and I give You a tenth of all I make.'*

---

* Translated from the Aramaic text.

¹³"But the despised tax collector stood off alone in the corner away from the Holy Place* and covered his face in his hands, feeling that he was unworthy to even look up to God. With brokenness and tears, he sobbed, 'God, please have mercy on me and because of the blood-sacrifice, forgive me,† for I am nothing but the most miserable of all sinners!'

¹⁴"Which one of them left for home that day made right with God? It was the humble tax collector and not the religious leader! For everyone that is proud and feels that they are superior to others will one day be humiliated before all; and everyone who humbles himself will one day be lifted up and honored before all!"

Jesus Blesses Children

¹⁵The people began to bring their babies and small children‡ to Jesus so that He might lay His hands on them to bless them. When the disciples saw this, it bothered them, so they scolded the parents and told them to stop troubling the Master. ¹⁶But Jesus called for the parents, the children, and His disciples to come and listen to Him. Then He told them, "Never hinder a child from coming to Me. Let them all come, for the kingdom-realm of God belongs to them as much as it does to anyone else! They demonstrate to you what faith is all about!§ ¹⁷Learn this well: Unless you receive the revelation of the kingdom-realm the same way a little child receives it, you will never be able to enter in!"

Jesus Speaks with a Young Wealthy Official ¶

¹⁸One day a wealthy Jewish nobleman of high standing, posed this question to Jesus: "Wonderful Teacher, what must I do to be saved and receive eternal life?" ¹⁹

Jesus answered, "Why would you call me wonderful when there is only One who is wonderful—and that is God alone?** ²⁰You already know what is right and what the commandments teach: 'Do not commit adultery, do not murder, do not steal, do not lie, and respectfully honor your father and your mother.'

---

* Implied in the text.
† Implied in the text. The Greek text uses a word that implies he was saying to God, "Look at me as You look at the blood sprinkled mercy-seat."
‡ There is a hint in the Greek text that these children may have been sick. Jesus loves and heals children!
§ Implied in the context, added for clarity.
¶ There is one ancient Christian tradition that says this was Saul of Tarsus, who became the Apostle Paul.
** Jesus is implying that if you call Him "wonderful" you are calling Him "God."

²¹The wealthy leader replied, "These are the very things I've been doing for as long as I can remember!"

²²"Ah," Jesus said, *"But there's still one thing you're missing in your life."*

"What is that?" asked the man.

*"You must go and sell everything that you own and give all the proceeds to the poor, and you will have eternal treasures. Then come and follow Me."**

²³But when the rich leader heard these words, he was devastated, for he was extremely wealthy.

²⁴Jesus saw his disappointment and looking right at him, He said, *"It is next to impossible for those who have everything to enter into the kingdom-realm of God!* ²⁵*Nothing could be harder! It could be compared to trying to stuff a camel through the eye of a needle!"†*

²⁶Those who heard this spoke up and said, "Then who can be saved?"

²⁷Jesus responded, *"What appears humanly impossible is more than possible with God. For God can do what man cannot!"*

²⁸Then Peter said, "Lord, see how we've left all that we have— our houses and our careers to follow You."

²⁹⁻³⁰Jesus replied, *"Listen to My words: Anyone who leaves their home behind and chooses the kingdom-realm of God over wife, children, parents and family— it will come back to them many more times in this lifetime; and in the age to come, they will inherit even more than that—they will inherit eternal life!"*

Jesus Prophesies His Death and Resurrection

³¹Jesus took the Twelve aside in private, and told them, *"We are going to Jerusalem so that everything prophesied about the Son of Man will be fulfilled.* ³²*They will betray Him and hand Him over to the people and they will mock Him, insult Him, and spit in His face.* ³³*And after they have abused‡ and flogged the Son of Man, they*

* This does not teach us that salvation can be earned by giving away our possessions to the poor. Jesus was showing the young wealthy man that he couldn't truly be a disciple until there was no competition in his heart in following Jesus.

† The words, "to stuff a camel through the eye of a needle" is a Hebrew metaphor for something impossible. The "eye of the needle" is a surgical word here in Luke. Imagine stuffing a camel through the eye of a needle! That humorous figure of speech was commonly used in that day. It would be like saying, "It's as hard as making pigs fly!"

‡ The word *abused* is powerful. It occurs in the Greek text in verse 32, but in the Aramaic text in verse 33.

will kill Him, but in three days He will rise again." ³⁴The disciples didn't have a clue about what He was saying, for His words were a mystery that was hidden from them.

Jesus Heals a Blind Beggar

³⁵As they arrived at Jericho, there was a blind beggar sitting on the roadside. ³⁶When he heard the crowd approaching, he asked, "What's all this commotion about?"

³⁷"It's Jesus! Jesus the Nazarene is passing by!" they said.

³⁸So the blind beggar shouted out, "Jesus, Son of David,* have pity and show me mercy!" ³⁹Those who were in the front of the crowd scolded him and warned him to be quiet. But the blind beggar screamed out even louder! "Jesus, Son of David, show me mercy!"

⁴⁰Suddenly, Jesus stopped and told those nearby, *"Bring the man over to Me."* When they brought him in front of Jesus, He asked the man, ⁴¹ *"What is it you want Me to do for you?"*

"Lord," he said, "Please, I want to see again!"

⁴²Jesus spoke these words to him, *"Now you will see! Receive your sight this moment! For your faith in Me has given you sight and new life!"*† ⁴³Instantly he could see again! His eyes popped opened, and he saw Jesus! He began to shout out loud praises to God and he followed Jesus! And when the crowd saw what happened, they too erupted with shouts of praise to God!

---

* The term, "Son of David" was used for the Messiah. The blind man believed Jesus was the Messiah.
† Translated from the Aramaic.

Luke 19

Jesus and Zacchaeus

¹⁻³In the city of Jericho there lived an extremely wealthy man named Zacchaeus who was the supervisor over all the tax collectors. As Jesus made His way through the city, Zacchaeus was eager to see Him. He kept trying to get a look at Him but the crowd around Jesus was massive, and Zacchaeus was a very short man and couldn't see over the heads of the people. ⁴So he ran on ahead of everyone and climbed up a blossoming fig tree* so he could get a glimpse of Jesus as He passed by.

⁵When Jesus got to that place He looked up in the tree and said, *"Zacchaeus, hurry on down, for I am appointed to stay† at your house today!"* ⁶He scurried down the tree and came face to face with Jesus. ⁷As Jesus left to go with Zacchaeus, many in the crowd began to complain, "Look at this! Of all the people to have dinner‡ with, He's going to eat in the house of a crook!"

⁸Zacchaeus joyously welcomed Jesus§ and was amazed over Jesus' gracious visit to his home. Then Zacchaeus stood up in front of the Lord and repented, "Half of all that I own I will give to the poor! And Lord, if I have cheated anyone of anything, I promise to pay them back four times as much as I stole!"

⁹⁻¹⁰Then Jesus said to him, *"This shows that today Life¶ has come to you and your household, for you are a true son of Abraham! The Son of Man has come to seek out and to give life to the lost!"***

---

* This was a sturdy sycamore-fig tree that was known to reach over forty feet high. The Aramaic text calls it a "tree in bloom."

† Although they had never met, Jesus knew his name. This was a "word of knowledge." The Aramaic text states, "It is My duty to stay at your house." It is likely that Jesus spent the night in the home of Zacchaeus.

‡ The Aramaic states, "dinner after the fast."

§ This is supplied from verse 6, stated here for the sake of the narrative.

¶ As translated from the Aramaic, the Greek text is, "salvation." Notice that Jesus describes Himself as "Life" and "Son of Man." He is both divine and human.

** This is a quotation taken from Ezekiel 34:16.

The Parable of a Prince and His Servants

[11]At this time Jesus was getting close to entering Jerusalem. The crowds that followed Him were convinced that the kingdom of God would fully manifest when Jesus established it in Jerusalem. [12]He told them this story to change their perspective: *"Once there was a wealthy prince who left his province to travel to a distant land where he was to be crowned king and then return.* [13]*Before the prince departed he summoned his ten servants together and said, 'I am entrusting each of you with $20,000* to trade with while I am away. Invest it and put the money to work until I return.'* [14]*But some of his countrymen despised the prince and sent a delegation after him to declare before the royals, 'We refuse to let this man rule over us! He will not be our king!'*

[15]*"Nevertheless, he was crowned king and returned to his land and summoned his ten servants to see how much each one had earned and what their profits came to.* [16]*The first one came forward and said, 'Master, I took what you gave me and invested it and it multiplied ten times!'* [17]*'Splendid! You have done well, my excellent servant! Because you have shown that you can be trusted in this small matter, I now grant you authority to rule over ten fortress cities!'* [18]*Then the second one came and said, 'Master what you left with me has multiplied five times.'* [19]*So his master said, 'I also grant you authority in my kingdom over five fortress cities!'* [20]*Then another came before the king and said, 'Master, here is the money you entrusted to me. I hid it for safe keeping.* [21]*You see, I live in fear of you, for everyone knows you are a strict master and impossible to please. You push us for a high return on all that you own and you always want to gain from someone else's efforts.†* [22]*So the king said to his servant, 'You wicked servant, I will judge you using your own words! If what you said about me is true, that I am a harsh man, pushing you for a high return and wanting gain from other's efforts—* [23]*why then didn't you at least put my money in the bank‡ to earn some interest on what I've entrusted to you?'*

[24]*"So the king said to his other servants, 'Take the money he has and give it to the faithful servant who multiplied my money ten times over!'* [25]*But master,' the other servants objected, 'Why give it to him? He already has so much!'* [26]*'Yes,' replied the king, 'but to all who have been faithful, even more will be given them! And for the ones who have nothing, even the little they seem to have will be taken from them.* [27]*Now*

---

* Literally, "ten minas."

† The text is literally; "you pick up what you didn't lay down and reap where you didn't sow." This statement is obviously not true. The opposite can be found in how the master shared his kingdom with the other more faithful servants. Many people today also have a misconception of the true heart of our "Master." Our Master makes servants into rulers.

‡ The text is literally, "upon a table," a metaphor for where banking transactions took place.

bring all those rebellious enemies of mine who rejected me as their king; bring them here before me and execute them!"

Jesus Enters Jerusalem

[28]After saying all of this, Jesus headed straight for Jerusalem. [29]When He arrived at the stables of Annia* near the Mount of Olives,[†] He sent two of His disciples ahead, saying, [30]*"As you enter the next village[‡] you will find a donkey's young colt that has never been ridden tethered there. Untie it and bring it to Me.* [31]*And if anyone stops you and asks, 'What are you doing?' Just tell them this: 'It is needed for the Lord of All.'"*[§]

[32]The two who were sent entered the village and found the colt exactly like Jesus had said! [33]While they were untying the colt the owners approached them and asked for an explanation, "What are you doing?"

[34]The disciples replied, "We need this donkey for the Lord of All!"

[35-36]So they brought the colt to Jesus, and they placed their prayer shawls on its back, and Jesus began to ride it as He descended the Mount of Olives toward Jerusalem.[¶] As He rode along, people spontaneously began to throw their prayer shawls on the path in front of Him like a carpet!"[**] [37]As soon as He got to the bottom of the Mount of Olives, the crowds of His followers began to shout out with a loud outburst of ecstatic joy over all the mighty wonders of power they had witnessed! [38]They shouted these words over and over: "Highest praises to God for the One who comes as King in the name of the Lord! Heaven's peace and glory from the highest realm now comes to us!"[††]

[39]But there were Jewish religious leaders that stood off from the procession who objected, and said to Jesus, "Teacher, you must order your followers at once to stop saying these things!"

[40]Jesus responded, *"Listen to Me, if My followers were silenced, the very stones would break forth with praises!"*

---

* The Greek text includes two small villages, "Bethphage" and "Bethany." The meaning of the names combined means, "the stables of Annia." This is how it is translated in the Aramaic.
† This was a large hill less than two miles from Jerusalem and about one hundred feet higher.
‡ Literally, "across the valley."
§ Implied, for the Lord Jesus created all things and therefore owns it all!
¶ See Zechariah 9:9.
** This was done to signify Jesus is King. See II Kings 9:13. This is an obvious reference to the coming of the promised Messiah.
†† Implied in the text. This is a quotation of Psalm 118:26.

Jesus Weeps Over Jerusalem

⁴¹When Jesus caught sight of the city, He burst into tears as He sobbed over Jerusalem, ⁴²saying, *"If you could only recognize that this day peace is within your reach, but you cannot see it!* ⁴³*For the day is soon coming when your enemies will surround you, pressing you in on every side, and laying siege to you!** ⁴⁴*They will crush you to pieces and your children too! And when they leave, your city will be totally destroyed! Since you would not recognize God's day of visitation, your day of devastation is coming!"*

Jesus Cleanses the Temple Courts

⁴⁵Then Jesus entered the temple area and began to forcibly throw out all the merchants from their stalls. ⁴⁶He rebuked them saying, *"The Scriptures declare: 'My Father's House is to be filled with prayer—a house of prayer*† *not a cave of bandits!'"*

⁴⁷From then on Jesus continued teaching in the temple area, but all the while, the high priests, the experts of the law, and the prominent men of the city kept trying to find a way they could accuse Jesus, for they wanted Him dead. ⁴⁸They could find no reason to accuse Him for He was a hero to the people and the crowds were awestruck by every word He spoke!

---

* Translated from the Aramaic, the Greek text states, "they will throw up ramparts." See Isaiah 29:3, Jeremiah 6:6 and Ezekiel 4:2.

† See Isaiah 56:7 and Jeremiah 7:11.

Luke 20

A Day of Controversy

¹One day Jesus was teaching in the temple courts and sharing with the people the wonderful news of salvation.* The high priest and the experts of the law were there with the prominent men of the city. They confronted Jesus and asked Him, ²"We want to know right now, by what authority you're doing this? Who gave you the authority to teach these things here in the temple?"

³Jesus responded, *"First, let me ask you a question and you tell me right now. ⁴Did John baptize because of a mandate from heaven or merely from men?"*

⁵His interrogators pulled aside to discuss it among themselves, "What should we say? If we say that John's mandate was from heaven, He will ask us, 'Then why didn't you believe him?' ⁶But if we say, 'John's mandate was merely from men,' then all the people around Him will stone us, for they believe John was a prophet of God."

⁷So they answered Jesus, "We cannot tell where John's authority came from."

⁸Jesus said, *"Then neither will I tell you where My authority comes from to do what I do!"*

The Story of the Vine-Growers

⁹Jesus taught the people this story: *"Once there was a man that planted a vineyard, then leased it out to tenants and left to go abroad and was away for a long time. ¹⁰When the harvest season arrived, the owner sent one of His servants to the tenants to collect the landowner's share of the harvest. But the tenants sent him away, beaten and empty-handed! ¹¹So the owner dispatched another one of his servants to collect his portion. But the tenants treated him the same way. They cursed him, beat him, and sent him away empty-handed. ¹²Then the owner sent a third servant, but they brutalized him with the same treatment. ¹³Finally the owner of the vineyard said to his son, 'Perhaps if I send you, my own cherished son, they will be ashamed of what*

---

* Translated from the Aramaic text.

they've done." [14]*But when the tenants saw the son coming they began to scheme among themselves, "This is the heir of the vineyard! If we kill him, the inheritance will be ours!'* [15]*So they threw him off the property and killed the son!*

"So I ask you, what do you think the owner of the vineyard will do to those who murdered his son? [16]*He will come and destroy them and give his vineyard to another!"*

When the people heard this story, they all agreed, "This should never happen!"

[17]But Jesus looked straight at the people and said, *"What do you think this verse actually means, 'The worthless, rejected stone, has become the Cornerstone, the most important stone of all?'[†]* [18]*Everyone who falls in humility[‡] upon that Stone will be broken! But if that Stone falls on you, it will grind you to pieces!"*

[19]When the high priests and experts of the law realized that this story was all about them, they wanted to have Him arrested that very moment, but they were afraid of all the people!

Paying Taxes

[20]They sent spies who pretended to be honest seekers, but they were watching closely for an opportunity to entangle Jesus by His words. Their plan was to catch Him saying something against the government and then they could hand Him over to the jurisdiction of the Roman authorities to be killed.[§] [21]At the right time they asked Him this question: "Teacher, we know that all You say is straightforward and what You teach us is right, giving us the true ways of God. You're One who doesn't show favoritism to anyone's status, so we ask You— [22]Is it proper or not to pay taxes to a corrupt government?"[¶]

[23]But Jesus saw right through their cunning ploy and said, *"Why are you testing me?"*[**] [24]*Show me one of the Roman coins. Whose head is on the coin? Whose title is stamped on it?"*

They answered, "Why, it's Caesar's."

---

* Translated from the Aramaic text.

† This is a quotation from Psalm 118:22. See also Isaiah 8:14-15 and Isaiah 28:16.

‡ Implied in the context.

§ The translator has chosen to make explicit what is implied about their plan and their desire that Jesus be killed.

¶ Implied in the context. The Greek text states, "to the Emperor."

** Although not found in most Greek manuscripts, it is included in the Aramaic text.

²⁵Jesus said, "*Precisely. The coin* bears the image of the Emperor Caesar, and you should give back to Caesar all that belongs to him. But you bear the image of God! So give back to God all that belongs to Him!*"²⁶The imposters were left speechless and amazed in the presence of all the people, unable to trap Jesus with His words.

A Question about the Resurrection

²⁷Some of the Sadducees, a religious group that denies there is a resurrection of the dead, came to ask Jesus this question: ²⁸"Teacher, the law of Moses† teaches that if a man dies before he has children, his brother should marry the widow and raise up children for his brother's family line. ²⁹But suppose there was a family with seven brothers and the oldest married and died without children. ³⁰⁻³¹Then his brother married the widow, but he too died with no children! And so it happened, one brother after another brother, until each of the seven had married the widow and died childless. ³²Finally, the widow died too. So here's our dilemma: ³³Whose wife will the woman be when she's resurrected from the dead? Which of the brothers will be her husband, for all seven were once married to her?"

³⁴Jesus replied, "*Marriage is for the sons of this world only.* ³⁵⁻³⁶*But those who are worthy of the resurrection from the dead into glory become immortal like the angels who never die nor marry. When the dead come to life again, they will be sons of God's life—the sons of the resurrection!* ³⁷*In fact, it was Moses who taught the resurrection of the dead‡ when he wrote of the Lord God who was at the burning bush and described Him as 'The God of Abraham, the God of Jacob, and the God of Isaac.'* ³⁸*Don't you agree that God is not the God of the dead, but the God of the living? For in His eyes, Abraham, Isaac, and Jacob are alive forevermore! He must be the God who raises the dead!*"

³⁹Then the experts of the law§ chimed in, "Yes, Teacher! You speak the truth beautifully!" ⁴⁰And from then on, the religious Sadducees never dared to ask Jesus a question again!

---

* Actual coins from that era have been found with the emperor's image and a superscription saying "Tiberius Caesar Augustus, son of the divine Augustus."
† See Deuteronomy 25:5-10.
‡ See Exodus 3:6.
§ Historically, these "experts of the law" (Pharisees) were opposed to, and argued with, the Sadducees over their unbelief of a supernatural resurrection.

The Messiah Will be Both God and Man

⁴¹Jesus then posed this question to them: *"How can the experts of the law* say that Christ the Messiah is David's son?* ⁴²*Haven't you read in the Psalms where David himself wrote,*

'The Lord Jehovah said to my Lord,†
"Sit near Me in the place of authority
⁴³*Until I subdue all Your enemies*
Under Your feet!"'‡

⁴⁴Jesus explained, *"So if David calls this One, 'my Lord,' then how can he merely be his son?"§*

Jesus Denounces the Experts of the Law

⁴⁵Within earshot of all the people, Jesus warned His disciples, ⁴⁶*"Don't follow the example of these pretentious experts of the law! They love to parade around in their clergy robes so that they are honored wherever they go, sitting right up front in every meeting and pushing for the head table at every banquet!* ⁴⁷*And for appearance's sake, they will pray long religious prayers at the homes of widows for an offering!¶ And they cheat them out of their very livelihood! Beware of them all, for they will one day be stripped of honor and the judgment they receive will be severe!"*

---

* Or "scribes," as translated from the Aramaic.

† A Hebrew translation of this passage would read, "Yahweh said to my Adonai." Paraphrased it would read, "The Lord (God) said to my protecting Lord (Messiah)."

‡ See Psalm 110:1. Translated from the Aramaic and one Greek manuscript. Most Greek texts have, "Until all Your enemies become a footstool under Your feet."

§ Jesus is challenging them to consider that the Christ will be both God and man—David's son and David's Lord.

¶ Translated from the Aramaic. The implication is that the religious leaders would go and pray at the homes of widows, then intimidate them and ask for offerings.

Luke 21

The Widow's Offering

¹Jesus was in the temple* observing all the wealthy wanting to be noticed as they came with their offerings. ²But then He noticed a very poor widow dropping her two small copper coins in the offering box. ³*"Listen to Me,"* He remarked, *"This poor widow has given a larger offering than any of the wealthy! ⁴For the rich only gave out of their surplus, but she sacrificed out of her poverty and gave to God all that she had to live on!"*

Jesus Prophesies the Signs of the End of the Age

⁵Some of the disciples began to remark about the beauty of the temple. They pointed out all the lovely adornments and how it was built with excellence from the gifts given to God. Jesus spoke up and said, ⁶*"The day will come that everything you admire here will be utterly destroyed—it will all become a heap of rubble!"*

⁷"Master, tell us," they asked, "When exactly will this happen? Can you tell us what warning sign to look for when it is about to take place?"

⁸Jesus responded, *"Deception will run rampant with many who will appear on the scene saying I have sent them, or to declare, 'I am the Messiah!'† And the doomsday deceivers will say, 'The end of the age is now here!' But listen to Me, don't be fooled by these imposters!*

⁹*"There will also be many wars and revolutions on every side, with rumors of more wars to come. Don't panic or give in to your fears, for these things are bound to happen! This is still not yet the end!"*

¹⁰Jesus continued, *"For there will be upheavals of every kind!‡ Nations will go to war against each other and kingdoms against kingdom—* ¹¹*and there*

---

* This would have been in the courtyard of the temple where men and women came to deposit their contributions in the temple treasury. Historians say there were thirteen trumpet-mouthed boxes used in the courtyard for offerings.
† Translated from the Aramaic it literally states, "I Am! The Messiah!"
‡ A summary statement implicit by the context.

will be terrible earthquakes, seismic events of epic proportion, resulting in famines in one place after another! There will be horrible plagues and epidemics, cataclysmic storms* on the earth, and astonishing signs and cosmic disturbances in the heavens. But before all of this happens, you will be hunted down and arrested—persecuted by both civil and religious authorities, and thrown into prison. ¹²⁻¹³And because you follow Me, you will be on trial before kings and governmental leaders as an opportunity to testify to them in My name. ¹⁴⁻¹⁵Yet determine in your heart not to prepare for your own defense, simply speak with the words of wisdom that I will give you that moment—and none of your persecutors will be able to withstand the grace and wisdom that comes from your mouth! ¹⁶You can expect betrayal by even your parents, your brothers, your relatives and friends—and yes, some of you will die as martyrs! ¹⁷You will be hated by all because of My life in you.† ¹⁸But don't worry. My grace will never desert you or depart from your life.‡ ¹⁹And by standing firm with patient endurance, you will find your souls' deliverance.

Jesus Prophesies the Destruction of Jerusalem§

²⁰"When you see Jerusalem being surrounded by armies, you will know for sure that its devastation is imminent. ²¹At that time all who are living in Judea must flee to the mountains! Those who live inside the city gates, go out and flee, and those who live outside the city must not enter it seeking refuge— ²²for these are the days of God's vengeance to fulfill what has been written¶ against Jerusalem. ²³It will be horrible for pregnant women and for those nursing little ones in that day, for there will be great persecution and wrath against this nation! ²⁴Many will be cut down by the sword or scattered as prisoners in many countries. And Jerusalem shall be trampled down by nations until the days of world empires come to an end.

The Coming of the Son of Man

²⁵"Expect to witness amazing and perplexing signs throughout the universe with the sun, the moon, and the stars.** And the raging of the sea will bring desperation and

---

* As translated from the Aramaic. Only one Greek manuscript adds, "great storms."

† Implied in the text. The Greek says, "because of My name."

‡ Although quite different from the Greek manuscripts, this is the literal translation of the Aramaic figure of speech, "grace will not leave your head."

§ This was fulfilled in 70 AD when Jerusalem was left desolate by Roman armies. Some historians estimate that over one million Jews were slaughtered at this time and up to 100,000 were taken captive to other nations.

¶ See 1 Kings 9:6-9, Daniel 9:26, Hosea 9:7, and Micah 3:12.

** See Isaiah 13:10, Ezekiel 32:7-8, and Joel 2:10.

turmoil to many nations. [26] Earthquakes* will bring panic and disaster. What men see coming to the earth will cause the fear of doom to grip their hearts, for they will even see the powers of the heavenly realm shaken! [27-28] And at last, when you see how the Son of Man† comes— surrounded with a cloud, with great power and miracles, and in the radiance of His splendor, and with great glory and praises,‡ it will make you jump for joy! For the day of your full transformation§ has arrived!"

The Lesson of the Fig Tree

[29-30] Jesus gave His disciples this parable: "Haven't you observed the fig tree, or any tree, that when they bud and bloom you realize that the season is changing and summer is near? [31] In the same way, when you see these prophetic signs occurring, you realize the earth is yielding to the fullness of the kingdom-realm of God! [32] I assure you, the end of this age will not come until all I have spoken comes to pass. [33] Earth and sky will wear out and fade away before one word I speak loses its power or fails to accomplish its purpose!

Guard Your Hearts

[34] "Be careful that you never allow your hearts to grow cold! Remain passionate ¶ and free from anxiety and the worries of this life. Then you will not be caught off guard by what happens. Don't let Me come and find you drunk or careless in living like everyone else! [35] For that day will come as a shocking surprise to all, like a downpour** that drenches everyone, catching many unaware and unprepared! [36] So keep a constant watch over your soul, and pray for the courage and grace to prevail over these things that are destined to occur, that you will stand before the presence of the Son of Man with a clear conscience."††

[37] Each day Jesus taught in the temple and would spend His nights on the Mount of Olives. [38] And all the people would come early to the temple courts to listen to the Manifestation of the Word‡‡ He taught.

---

* The word *earthquakes* is found only in Aramaic manuscripts.
† The title, "Son of Man" was used frequently when Jesus spoke of Himself. Note that He is not the "son of a man," but the Son who became man.
‡ "Praises" is only found in Aramaic manuscripts.
§ The Greek word is "redemption" or "liberation." It speaks of the total transformation of our body, soul, and spirit when we see Him as He is!
¶ The Aramaic text says, "Beware that your heart never grows cold."
** Greek manuscripts have, "like a snare." The Aramaic text states, "like a downpour."
†† Implied in the context.
‡‡ The Greek text is *logos*. The Aramaic is literally, "Manifestation."

Luke 22

Satan Entered into Judas

¹⁻²As the celebration of the Passover lamb* was approaching, the Jewish religious leaders and scholars of the law were continually scheming to find a way they could murder Jesus without starting a riot—for they feared the crowds. ³At that time Satan himself entered into Judas the locksmith,† who was one of the twelve apostles. ⁴He secretly went to the religious hierarchy and the captains of the temple guards to discuss with them how he could betray Jesus and turn Him over to their hands. ⁵The religious hierarchy was elated over Judas' treachery, so they agreed to give him a sum of money in exchange for Jesus' betrayal. ⁶Judas vowed that he would find them a suitable opportunity to betray Jesus when He was away from the crowds.

Jesus Prophesies the Location of the Last Supper

⁷⁻⁸On the day the sacrifices of the Passover lambs was to take place, Jesus sent for Peter and John and instructed them: *"Go and prepare the Passover supper so we can eat it together."*

⁹They asked Him, "Where do we make the preparations to eat the meal?"

¹⁰Jesus gave them this sign, *"When you enter the city, you will find a man‡ carrying a jug of water; follow him home* ¹¹*and say to the owner of the house, 'The Teacher told us to ask you, "Where is the room I may use to have the Passover meal with My disciples?"'* ¹²*He will then take you to a large, fully furnished upstairs room. Make the preparations for us there."* ¹³So they went and found everything to be exactly like Jesus had prophesied and they prepared the Passover meal.

---

* The Passover celebration was known as the "Feast of Bread without yeast." The Jewish people commemorate their exodus from Egypt to this day with a week long Passover Feast. See Exodus 12:1-20 and Deuteronomy 16:1-8.

† See footnote on Luke 6:14-16.

‡ Carrying water was the task given to women; it would have been easy to spot a man carrying the water jug.

Jesus and His Disciples Eat the Last Supper

[14]When Jesus arrived to the upper room He took His place at the table along with all the apostles. [15]Then He told them, *"I have longed with passion and desire to eat this Passover lamb with you before I endure my sufferings.* [16]*I can promise you that the next time we eat this we will be together in the banquet of the kingdom-realm of God."* [17]Then He raised a cup and gave thanks to God and said to them, *"Take this and pass it on to one another and drink.* [18]*I can promise you that the next time we drink this wine we will be together in the feasting of the kingdom-realm of God."'* [19]Then He lifted up a loaf and after praying a prayer of thanksgiving to God, He gave each of His apostles a piece of bread, saying, *"This loaf is My body which is now being offered to you. Always eat it to remember Me."* [20]And after supper was over, He lifted the cup again and said, *"This cup is My blood of the new covenant[†] I make with you, and it will be poured out soon for all of you.* [21]*But I want you to know that the hands of the one who delivers Me to be the sacrifice are with Mine on the table this very moment.* [22]*The Son of Man must now go where He will be sacrificed. But there will be great and unending doom for the man who betrays Me.* [23]And the apostles immediately began to question among themselves which one of them was about to do this.

The Apostle Argue Over Which of Them Will be the Greatest

[24]Then the disciples began to bicker over which one of them would be considered the greatest[‡] in the kingdom. [25]And Jesus interrupted their argument, saying, *"The kings and men of authority in this world rule oppressively over their subjects, claiming that they do it for the good of the people. They are obsessed with how others see them.[§]* [26]*But this is not your calling. You will lead by a different model. The greatest one among you will live as one called to serve others without honor![¶] The greatest honor and authority is reserved for the one that has a servant-heart.* [27]*You think that the leaders who are served are the most important in your eyes, but in the kingdom, it is the servants who lead. Am I not here with you as One who serves you?*

---

* Verses 17-18 are not found in most Aramaic texts. Most Greek texts and a fifth century Aramaic manuscript known as, "The Palestinian Syriac," include them in the narrative.

† The Aramaic word used here is literally, "New Testament."

‡ This took place at the Lord's Passover table. Their discussion of who was the worst among them lead them to argue over who was the greatest. Jesus was only hours away from the horrible death of crucifixion while His apostles argued.

§ The Aramaic is actually, "they want to be called, servants of goodness."

¶ The Greek text uses the word here for "youngest" and the Aramaic uses the words, "small one." In Hebrew culture in the days of Jesus, it was the firstborn of the household who had honor, while the youngest accepted the role of menial service to all the others of the house.

Twelve Thrones

²⁸*"Because you have stood with Me through all My trials and ordeals,* ²⁹*I give you your destiny:* I am promising you the kingdom that the Father has promised Me!* ³⁰*We will celebrate in this kingdom-realm and you will feast with Me at My table. And each of you will be given a throne—twelve thrones, and you will be made rulers on thrones to judge the tribes of Israel.*

Jesus Prophesies of Peter's Denial

³¹*"Peter, My dear friend—listen to what I'm about to tell you. Satan has demanded to come and sift you all like wheat and test your faith.* ³²*But I have prayed for you, Peter, that you would stay faithful to Me no matter what comes! Remember this: After you have turned back to Me and have been restored, make it your life mission to strengthen the faith of your brothers!"*

³³"But Lord," Peter replied, "I am ready to stand with you to the very end, even if it means prison or death!"

³⁴Jesus looked at him and prophesied, *"Before the rooster crows in the morning you will deny*† *that you even know Me three times!"*

³⁵Then He said to all of them, *"When I sent you out empty-handed, did you lack anything?"*

They answered, "Not a thing! God provided all we needed!" *"But now I say to you: Take what you need.* ³⁶*If you have money, take it— and a knapsack, and a sword! Danger is imminent!*‡ ³⁷*For the prophetic Scripture about Me, 'He will be accused of being a criminal,' will now come to pass. All that was prophesied of Me will be fulfilled!"*

³⁸And the disciples told Him, "Lord, we already have two swords!"

"That will be enough," Jesus responded.

The Garden of Gethsemane

³⁹Then Jesus left the upper room with His disciples,§ and as was His habit, went to the Mount of Olives, His place of secret prayer.⁹ ⁴⁰There He told them, *"Keep on praying for strength to be spared from the severe test of your*

---

* Implied in the context.
† The Aramaic text say, "blasphemed."
‡ The words of the text here are a Hebraic figure of speech, "if you don't have a sword, sell something and buy one," which means, "danger is imminent."
§ That is, with the exception of Judas. See verse 47.
¶ Implied in the context.

faith that is about to come." ⁴¹Then He withdrew from them a short distance* to be alone. Kneeling down, He prayed: ⁴²*"Father, if You are willing, take this cup of agony away from Me.*† *But no matter what, Your will must be done, not Mine!"* ⁴³Just then, He called‡ for an angel of glory to strengthen Him, and the angel appeared. ⁴⁴He prayed even more passionately, like One being sacrificed,§ until He was in such intense agony of spirit that His sweat became drops of blood dripping onto the ground!¶ ⁴⁵When Jesus finished praying, He got up and went to His disciples and found them all asleep, for they were exhausted and overwhelmed with sorrow! ⁴⁶*"Why are you sleeping?"* He asked them, *"You need to be alert and pray for the strength to endure the great temptation."*

Judas Betrays Jesus

⁴⁷No sooner had He finished speaking when suddenly a mob approached, and right in front of the mob was His disciple, Judas! He walked up close to Jesus and greeted Him with a kiss. For he had agreed to give them a sign, saying, "The One I kiss is the One to seize!"**⁴⁸But Jesus looked at him with sorrow, and said, *"A kiss, Judas? Are you really going to betray the Son of Man with a kiss?"* ⁴⁹When the other disciples understood what was happening, they asked, "Lord, shall we fight them with our swords?" ⁵⁰Just then, one of the disciples†† swung his sword at the High Priest's servant and slashed off his right ear!

⁵¹But Jesus stopped it from escalating any further by shouting out, *"Stop! That's enough of this!"* Then He touched the right side of the injured man's head and the ear grew back—‡‡he was healed! ⁵²Jesus turned to those who had come to seize Him: the ruling priests, the officers of the temple police, and the religious leaders, and said: *"Am I a criminal that you would come to capture Me with clubs and swords? Wasn't I with you day after*

---

* Literally, "a stone's throw away."

† Jesus was asking the Father to be spared from death in the garden so that He could go all the way to the cross—His prayer was answered. The blood that dripped in the garden would not redeem; He must carry the cross and fulfill all that was written of Him. See Hebrews 5:7.

‡ Translated from the Aramaic text. The Greek manuscripts state it passively, "an angel from heaven appeared."

§ The Aramaic text is literally, "He prayed sacrificially."

¶ Verses 43-44, although found in the Aramaic manuscript, many Greek texts omit them. Most of the early church fathers included them in their translations and commentaries.

** Nearly every Greek manuscript leaves out this information. The Aramaic text includes it.

†† The unnamed disciple was Peter, the servant's name was Malchus. See John 18:10.

‡‡ Implied in the context of this miracle. Jesus, the Creator, re-created his ear.

day teaching in the temple courts? [53]*You could have seized Me at any time! But in the darkness of night you have now found your time, for it belongs to you and to the Prince of Darkness!"**

Peter Denies Knowing Jesus

[54]Then they seized Jesus and led Him away, but Peter followed them from a safe distance. They brought Him to the home of the High Priest where people were already gathered outside in the courtyard. [55]Someone had built a fire so Peter inched closer and sat down among them to stay warm. [56]Soon a girl noticed it was Peter sitting there in the firelight! Staring at him, she pointed him out and said, "This man is one of Jesus' disciples!"

[57]But Peter flatly denied it and said, "What are you talking about girl? I don't know Him!"

[58]A little while later, someone else spotted Peter and asserted, "I recognize you! You're one of His; I know it!"

Peter again spoke out, "I'm not one of His disciples!"

[59]Then about an hour later someone else identified Peter and insisted he was a disciple of Jesus, saying, "Look at him! He's from Galilee[†] just like Jesus! I know He's one of them!"

[60]But Peter was adamant, "Listen, I don't know what you're talking about! Don't you understand? I don't even know Him!" While the words were still in his mouth, the rooster crowed.

[61]At that very moment, the Lord was being led through the courtyard by His captors.[‡] He heard it all and turned around and gazed at Peter! All at once Peter remembered the words Jesus had prophesied over him, "*Before the rooster crows in the morning three times you will deny that you even know Me!*" [62]Peter burst into tears, ran off from the crowd and wept bitterly!

Jesus is Mocked and Severely Beaten

[63]Those who were guarding Jesus began to mock and beat Him severely! [64]They also made fun of Him, blindfolding Him and slapping His face saying, "Prove that You are a prophet and tell us which one

---

* The "Prince of Darkness" is Satan. This phrase is only found in the Aramaic manuscripts. The Greek text states, "the powers of darkness."

† It was Peter's accent that gave him away as being a Galilean. See also Mark 14:70.

‡ Implied by the context, necessary for proper understanding of the narrative.

of us hit You!" ⁶⁵They continued to blaspheme and heaped insult after insult upon Him.

Jesus before the Jewish Council

⁶⁶At daybreak the High Priests, the experts of the law, and the top religious leaders convened together and had Jesus brought before their council. ⁶⁷They asked Him point blank, "Tell us, are You the Christ, the Messiah, or not!"

Jesus responded, *"If I tell you the truth, you won't believe Me;* ⁶⁸*and if I question you, you will not answer Me or release Me.** ⁶⁹*But from today on, the Son of Man will be enthroned in the place of honor, power, and authority with Almighty God."*

⁷⁰They all shouted, "Then You claim to be the Son of God?"

And He said to them, *"You are the ones that say I AM!"*

⁷¹Then they all shouted out, "We've heard it from His very lips! What further proof do we need?"

---

* The phrase, "or release Me" is found only in the Aramaic text.

Luke 23

Jesus before Pilate

¹Then the entire council stood up at once and took Jesus to Pilate, the Roman governor. ²And they accused Him with false testimony before the governor saying, "This Man tells us that we're not to pay our taxes to Caesar! And He proclaims Himself to be Christ the King and Messiah! He's a deceiver of our nation!"

³Then Pilate asked Him, "Is this true? Are You their King and Messiah?"

Jesus answered, "*It is true.*"

⁴Then Pilate turned to the High Priests and to the gathered crowd, "This Man has committed no crime. I find nothing wrong with Him."

⁵But they yelled and demanded Pilate to do something, saying, "He has stirred up our nation, misleading people from the moment He began teaching in Galilee until He has come here to Jerusalem!"

Jesus before Herod

⁶⁻⁷When Pilate heard the word *Galilee*, he asked if Jesus was a Galilean, as he knew that Herod was the ruler over Galilee. When they told him yes, Pilate saw a way out of his problem. Herod just so happened to be in Jerusalem at that time, so Pilate sent Jesus to Herod. ⁸When Herod saw Jesus he was elated, for he had heard a great deal about His ministry and wanted Jesus to perform a miracle in front of him. ⁹Herod questioned Him at length, but Jesus wouldn't even answer him. ¹⁰⁻¹¹All the while the High Priests and religious leaders stood by hatefully accusing Jesus of wrongdoing, so that even Herod and his soldiers began to treat Him with scorn and mocking. Then Herod put an elegant purple robe on Jesus and sent Him back to Pilate. ¹²That very day Herod and Pilate healed the rift between themselves due to old hostilities, and they became good friends.

Jesus Sentenced to Death

13-14Then Pilate gathered the people together with the high priests and all the religious leaders of the nation* and told them: "You have presented this Man to me and charged Him with stirring a rebellion among the people. But I say to you that I have examined Him here in your presence and have put Him on trial. My verdict is that none of the charges you have brought against Him are true. I find no fault in Him.† 15-16And I sent Him to Herod who also, after questioning Him, has found Him not guilty. Since He has done nothing deserving of death, I have now decided to punish Him with a severe flogging and release Him." 17For it was Pilate's custom to honor the Jewish holiday by releasing a prisoner.‡

18When they heard this, the entire crowd went wild; erupting with anger, they cried out, "No! Take this One away and release Barabbas!" 19For Barabbas had been thrown in prison for robbery§ and murder.

20Again Pilate, wanting to release Jesus, tried to convince them it was best to let Jesus go. 21But they cried out over and over, "Crucify Him! Crucify Him!"¶

22Then, for the third time, Pilate told the crowd, "What evil crime has this Man committed that I should have Him crucified? I haven't found one thing that warrants a death sentence! I will have Him flogged severely and then release Him and let Him go."

23But the people and the High Priests, shouting like a mob, screamed out at the top of their lungs, "No! Crucify Him! Crucify Him!" And finally their shouts and screams succeeded!

24Pilate caved in to the crowd and ordered that the will of the people be done. 25Then he released the guilty murderer Barabbas as they had insisted, and handed Jesus over to be crucified.

The Crucifixion of Jesus

26As they led Jesus to be crucified there was a black man** in the crowd named Simon, a North African†† who had just arrived from a rural village

---

* This group of religious leaders was known as the Jewish council of the Sanhedrin.
† The phrase, "I find no fault in Him," is found in the Aramaic text.
‡ Although many Greek manuscripts do not have this verse included in the text, it is found in the Aramaic text.
§ Most Greek manuscripts have, "for insurrection." The Aramaic states, "for robbery."
¶ Crucifixion was the cruelest form of execution, reserved only for the worst of criminals.
** Implied by being a native of Africa.
†† The text is literally, "from Cyrene," which is present day Tripoli, Libya.

to keep the Feast of Passover.* They laid the cross on his shoulders† and forced Simon to walk behind Jesus and carry His cross. ²⁷Massive crowds gathered to follow Jesus including a number of women who were wailing with sorrow over Him. ²⁸But Jesus turned to them and said, *"Daughters of Jerusalem, do not weep for Me. You should be weeping for yourselves and your children.* ²⁹*For the day is coming when it will not be the women with children who are blessed, but the childless. Then you will say, 'The barren women are the most fortunate! Those who have never given birth and never nursed a child—they are more fortunate than we are, for they will never see their children put to death!'‡* ³⁰*And the people will begin to cry out for the mountains and hills to fall on top of them to hide them from all that is to come!§* ³¹*For if this is what they do to the Living Branch,¶ what will they do with the dead ones!"*

³²Two criminals were also led away with Jesus; all three were to be executed together. ³³When they came to the place that is known as "The Skull" they crucified Jesus there, nailing Him on the center cross between the two criminals. ³⁴And while they were nailing Jesus to the cross, He prayed, *"Father, forgive them, for they don't even know what they are doing."* The soldiers, after they crucified Him, gambled over His clothing.**

³⁵By now the crowd gathered to watch what was happening but the religious leaders sneered at Jesus and mocked Him by saying, "Look at this Man! What kind of 'Chosen Messiah' is this? He pretended to save others, but He can't even save Himself!"

³⁶Then the soldiers joined in the mockery by offering Him a drink of vinegar!†† ³⁷⁻³⁸And over Jesus' head on the cross there was written an inscription in Greek, Latin, and Aramaic:‡‡ "This man is the King of all the Jews." So all the soldiers laughed and scoffed at Him saying, "Hey! If You're the 'King of the Jews,' why don't You save Yourself?"

³⁹One of the criminals hanging on the cross next to Jesus kept ridiculing Him over and over saying, "What kind of Messiah are You? Save Yourself and save us from this death!"

---

* Implied in the text.
† By this time Jesus had been severely beaten and flogged, without sleep, and carrying a heavy load. It is assumed this is why Simon was compelled to carry the cross for Him.
‡ Implied in the context to convey the meaning of the text.
§ See Hosea 10:8.
¶ The Aramaic is literally, "a green tree." This could be a figure of speech for "an innocent man." The "dead" could be a figure of speech for "an evil man."
** Many Greek manuscripts have unfortunately omitted verse 34.
†† See Psalm 69:21. It was likely Jesus had nothing to drink since the night before.
‡‡ Many Greek texts omit the mention of these three languages.

⁴⁰But the criminal hanging on the other cross rebuked the man and said, "Don't you fear God? You're about to die! ⁴¹We deserve to be condemned for we're just being repaid for what we've done! But this Man—He's done nothing wrong!"

⁴²Then he said, "I beg of You, My Lord Jesus, show me grace and take me with You into Your everlasting* kingdom!"

⁴³Jesus responded, saying, *"I promise you—this very day you will enter Paradise with Me."*

The Death of the Savior

⁴⁴It was now only midday yet the whole world became dark for three hours as the light of the sun faded away!† ⁴⁵Then suddenly in the temple, the thick veil hanging in the Holy Place was ripped in two! ⁴⁶Then Jesus cried out with a loud voice—*"Father, I surrender My Spirit into Your hands!"*‡ And He took His last breath and died!

⁴⁷When the Roman captain overseeing the crucifixion witnessed all that took place, he was awestruck and began to glorify God! Acknowledging what they had done, he said, "I have no doubt; we just killed the Righteous One!"§

⁴⁸And the crowds that had gathered to observe this spectacle went back to their homes overcome with deep sorrow,¶ and were totally devastated by what they had witnessed! ⁴⁹But standing off at a distance were some who truly knew Jesus and the women who had followed Him all the way from Galilee were keeping vigil.

⁵⁰⁻⁵¹There was also a member of the Jewish council named Joseph from the city of Arimathea—a good hearted, honorable man who was eager for the appearing of the kingdom-realm of God. He had not agreed at all with the decision of the council to crucify Jesus.** ⁵²He came before Pilate and asked permission to take the body of Jesus and give Him a proper burial, so Pilate granted his request.†† ⁵³He took the body from

---

* Implied in the context.
† This indicates the "day of the Lord" has now come. See Joel 2:10 and Amos 8:9.
‡ See Psalm 22:1 and Psalm 31:5.
§ As translated from the Aramaic.
¶ Literally, "beating their breasts," which is a figure of speech for deep sorrow.
** One ancient Syrian manuscript adds here, "This man was one who did not take part with the mind of the Devil."
†† Implied in the text.

the cross, wrapped it in a winding sheet of linen, and placed it in a new, unused tomb chiseled out of solid rock. [54]It was the Preparation Day, and the Sabbath was fast approaching. [55]The women who had been companions of Jesus from the beginning saw all this take place and watched as the body was laid in the tomb. [56]Afterwards they returned home and prepared sweet spices and ointments and were planning to anoint His body after the Sabbath was completed, according to the commandments of the Law.

Luke 24

The Resurrection of Jesus

¹Very early that Sunday morning, the women made their way to the tomb carrying the spices they had prepared. Among them was Mary Magdalene, Joanna, and Mary, Jesus' mother, along with others.* ²Arriving at the tomb they discovered that the huge stone covering the entrance had been rolled aside, ³so they went in to look—but the tomb was empty! The body of Jesus was gone! ⁴They stood there stunned and perplexed, when suddenly two men in dazzling white robes shining like lightning appeared above them!† ⁵Terrified, the women fell to the ground on their faces.

The men in white said to them, "Why would you look for the Living One in a tomb?‡ He is not here, for He has risen! ⁶Have you forgotten what He said to you while He was still in Galilee: ⁷*The Son of Man is destined to be handed over to sinful men to be nailed to a cross, and on the third day He will rise again!'*"

⁸All at once they remembered His words! ⁹Leaving the tomb they went to break the news to the eleven and to all the others of what they had seen and heard!§ ¹¹But when the disciples heard the testimony of the women, it seemed to make no sense at all and they were unable to believe what they heard.

¹²All at once Peter jumped up and ran the entire distance to the tomb to see for himself! And stooping down, he looked inside and discovered it was empty! There was only the linen sheet lying there! Staggered by this, he walked away wondering to himself what it meant.

---

* For the sake of the English narrative, the information found in verse 10 is placed here.
† "Above them" is found only in the Aramaic text.
‡ The Aramaic text is literally, "The Life."
§ For the sake of the English narrative, the information of verse 10 is included in verse 1.

Jesus Walks to Emmaus

¹³Later that Sunday, two of His disciples were walking from Jerusalem to Emmaus,* a journey of about seven miles. ¹⁴⁻¹⁵They were in the midst of a discussion about all the events of the last few days when Jesus walked up and accompanied them in their journey. ¹⁶Yet they were totally unaware that it was Jesus walking alongside of them, for God prevented them from recognizing Him!

¹⁷⁻¹⁸Jesus said to them, *"You seem to be in a deep discussion about something. What are you talking about, so sad and gloomy?"* Immediately they stopped, and the one named, Cleopas,† finally answered Him, "Haven't you heard? Are you the only one in Jerusalem unaware of the things that have happened over the last few days?"

¹⁹Jesus asked them, *"What things?"*

"The things about Jesus, the Man from Nazareth," they replied. "He was a mighty Prophet of God who performed miracles and wonders. His words were powerful and He had great favor with God and the people. ²⁰⁻²¹But three days ago the High Priests and the rulers of the people sentenced Him to death and had Him crucified. We all hoped that He was the One who was going to redeem and rescue Israel. ²²Early this morning, some of the women informed us of something amazing. ²³They said they went to the tomb earlier this morning, and found it empty. They claimed two angels appeared, and told them that Jesus is now alive. ²⁴So some of us went to see for ourselves and found the tomb exactly like the women had said—but no one has seen Him!"

²⁵Then Jesus said to them, *"Why are you so thick-headed? Why do you find it so hard to believe every word the prophets have spoken? ²⁶Wasn't it necessary for Christ, the Messiah, to experience all these sufferings and then afterwards, He would enter into His glory?"*

²⁷Then Jesus carefully unveiled before them the revelation of Himself throughout the Scripture. He started from the beginning and explained the writings of Moses and all the prophets, showing how they wrote of Him and revealed the truth about Himself before their

---

* Emmaus was a village about seven miles northwest of Jerusalem. The word *Emmaus* is taken from a Hebrew root that means, "the burning place."

† *Cleopas* means, "of a renowned father." Some scholars believe this could also be the Clopas mentioned in John 19:25. Interestingly, *Cleopas* is a Hebrew feminine word and is likely a woman's name. Some have even speculated that Cleopas was the wife of Peter.

very eyes! ²⁸As they approached the village, Jesus walked on ahead telling them He was going on to a distant place.

²⁹But they urged Him to stay and pleaded with Him to remain there, "Stay with us," they insisted, "It will be dark soon." So Jesus went with them into the village. ³⁰Joining them at the table for supper, He took bread and blessed it and broke it, and gave it to them. ³¹All at once their eyes were opened and they realized it was Jesus! Then suddenly, in a flash, Jesus vanished from before their eyes!

³² Stunned, they looked at each other and said, "Why didn't we recognize it was Him? Weren't our hearts burning with the flames of holy passion* while we walked beside Him listening to such profound revelation from the Scriptures? ³³Then they left at once and hurried back to Jerusalem to tell the other disciples! When they found the eleven and the other disciples all together, ³⁴they overheard them saying, "It's really true! The Lord has risen from the dead! He even appeared to Peter!" ³⁵Then the two disciples told the others what had happened to them on the road to Emmaus and how Jesus had unveiled Himself as He broke bread with them!

Jesus Appears to the Disciples

³⁶⁻³⁷While they were still discussing all of this, Jesus suddenly manifested right in front of their eyes! Startled and terrified, the disciples were convinced they were seeing a ghost! Standing there among them He said, *"Be at peace! I am the Living God; don't be afraid!*† ³⁸*Why would you be so frightened? Don't let doubt or fear*‡ *enter your hearts, for I AM!* ³⁹*Come and gaze upon My pierced hands and feet! See for yourselves; it is I, standing here alive! Touch Me, and know that I am not a ghost! See, I have a body of flesh and bone!"* ⁴⁰Then He showed them His pierced hands and feet and let them touch His wounds.§ ⁴¹They were ecstatic, yet dumbfounded, unable to fully comprehend it! Knowing that they were still wondering if He was real, Jesus said, *"Here, let Me show you—give Me something to eat."*

---

* As translated from the Greek text. The Aramaic manuscript reads quite differently, stating, "Were not our hearts dull as He taught us." This is also the translation of the Latin text. The Aramaic word for "burning" and for "dull" are almost identical.
† The words, "I am the Living God, don't be afraid" are only found in the Aramaic text and the Latin Vulgate. The Greek text omits this sentence.
‡ The Aramaic read, "imaginations."
§ Verse 40 is missing in some manuscripts.

⁴²⁻⁴³So they handed Him a piece of broiled fish and some honeycomb. And they watched Jesus eat it right in front of their eyes!

⁴⁴Then He said to them, *"Don't you remember the words that I spoke to you when I was still with you? I told you that everything written about Me would be fulfilled including all the prophecies from the law of Moses through the Psalms and the writings of the prophets—they would all find their fulfillment in what has happened!"* ⁴⁵Then He supernaturally unlocked their understanding* to receive the revelation of the Scriptures, ⁴⁶and said to them, *"Everything that has happened fulfills what was prophesied of Me. Christ, the Messiah, was destined to suffer and rise from the dead on the third day.* ⁴⁷*Now you must go into all the nations and preach salvation's grace† and forgiveness of sins so that they will turn to Me! Start right here in Jerusalem.* ⁴⁸*For you are My witnesses and have seen for yourselves all that has transpired.* ⁴⁹*And I will send the fulfillment of the Father's promise‡ to you! So stay here in the city until the mighty power of heaven falls upon you and wraps around you!"*

The Ascension of Jesus

⁵⁰Then Jesus led His disciples out to Bethany and He lifted up His hands over them to bless them in His love. ⁵¹While He was still speaking words of love and blessing, He began to float off the ground into the sky, ascending into heaven before their very eyes! ⁵²All they could do was worship Him! Overwhelmed and ecstatic with joy, they finally made their way back to Jerusalem. ⁵³Every day you could find them in the temple praising and worshipping God!

---

* Implied in the text.
† The Aramaic reads, "grace" or "conversion."
‡ The Aramaic reads, "the kingdom" or "rule." The "Father's promise" would be the coming of the Holy Spirit to live in them and empower them. See Acts 2:1-12.

And so ends the glorious gospel of Luke. The one who walked with His friends on the way to Emmaus wants to walk with us! May we never walk in sadness or unbelief for He is raised from the grave and lives victorious as the Living God in resurrection life! May you pause here and rejoice, believing that Jesus is the Christ, the Son of the Living God and the only One that will bring us to the Father. Trust in Him alone to save you, and you will spend eternity with Him!

About the Translator

Dr. Brian Simmons has previously been involved in the translation project of the Kuna New Testament and has studied linguistics and Bible translation principles through New Tribes Mission. He and his family spent nearly eight years in the tropical rain forest of the Darien Province of Panama, as a church planter, translator, and consultant. Afterward, he assisted in planting a thriving church in West Haven, CT—Gateway Christian Fellowship. Brian now travels full time as a conference speaker and Bible teacher. You may bump into him someday on a flight somewhere with his laptop, working on the Passion Translation. Brian has been married for forty years and boasts regularly of his three children and six grandchildren. He and his wife, Candice, make their home in Wichita, Kansas. He may be contacted at:

brian@passiontranslation.com

For more information about the translation project or any of Brian's books, please visit: www.stairwayministries.org or www.passiontranslation.com, or search for him on Facebook and Twitter.

More from *The Passion Translation*

The Most Amazing Song of All
by Brian Simmons
ISBN: 978-1-936578-03-0
$9.00

Breathtaking and beautiful, we see the Shulamite's sojourn unveiled in this anointed allegory. It becomes a journey that not only describes the divine parable penned by Solomon, but one that every longing lover of Jesus will find as his or her very own.

In this new Passion Translation™, the translator uses the language of the heart, passionate and loving, to translate the book from Hebrew to English.

More from *The Passion Translation*

The Psalms, Poetry on Fire
by Brian Simmons
ISBN: 978-1-936578-28-3
$17.00

The Psalms, Poetry on Fire translated by Dr. Brian Simmons find the words that express our deepest and strongest emotions. The Psalms will turn your sighing into singing and your trouble into triumph. No matter what you may be going through in your life, the Psalms have a message for you! As you read these 150 poetic masterpieces, your heart will be stirred to worship God in greater ways.

5 Fold Media, LLC is a Christ-centered media company. Our desire is to produce lasting fruit in writing, music, art, and creative gifts.

"To Establish and Reveal"
For more information visit:
www.5foldmedia.com

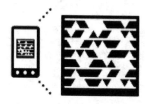

Use your mobile device to scan the tag above and visit our website.
Get the free app: http://gettag.mobi

Like 5 Fold Media on Facebook, follow us on Twitter!